ations

534   621.385

Series Editor: David Sang

CAMBRIDGE
UNIVERSITY PRESS

PUBLISHED BY THE PRESS SYNDICATE OF THE UNIVERSITY OF CAMBRIDGE
The Pitt Building, Trumpington Street, Cambridge, United Kingdom

CAMBRIDGE UNIVERSITY PRESS
The Edinburgh Building, Cambridge CB2 2RU, UK
40 West 20th Street, New York, NY 10011-4211, USA
10 Stamford Road, Oakleigh, VIC 3166, Australia
Ruiz de Alarcón 13, 28014 Madrid, Spain
Dock House, The Waterfront, Cape Town 8001, South Africa

http://www.cambridge.org

First published 2001

Printed in the United Kingdom at the University Press, Cambridge

Typeface   Swift   *System*   QuarkXPress®

A catalogue record for this book is available from the British Library

ISBN 0 521 79747 0 paperback

Produced by Gecko Ltd, Bicester, Oxon

Front cover photographs: Hanbury Brown radio telescope at Sunset,
Australia, Science Photo Library

Contents

Introduction

Cambridge Advanced Sciences

The *Cambridge Advanced Sciences* series has been developed to meet the demands of all the new AS and A level science examinations. In particular, it has been endorsed by OCR as providing complete coverage of their specifications. The AS material is presented as a single text for each of biology, chemistry and physics. Material for the A2 year comprises six books in each subject: one of core material and one for each option. Some material has been drawn from the existing *Cambridge Modular Sciences* books; however, the majority is entirely new.

During the development of this series, the opportunity has been taken to improve the design, and a complete and thorough new writing and editing process has been applied. Much more material is now presented in colour. Although the existing *Cambridge Modular Sciences* texts do cover some of the new specifications, the *Cambridge Advanced Sciences* books cover every OCR learning objective in detail. They are the key to success in the new AS and A level examinations.

OCR is one of the three unitary awarding bodies offering the full range of academic and vocational qualifications in the UK. For full details of the new specifications, please contact OCR:

OCR, 1 Hills Road, Cambridge CB1 2EU
Tel: 01223 553311

The presentation of units

You will find that the books in this series use a bracketed convention in the presentation of units within tables and on graph axes. For example, ionisation energies of $1000\,\text{kJ}\,\text{mol}^{-1}$ and $2000\,\text{kJ}\,\text{mol}^{-1}$ will be represented in this way:

Measurement	Ionisation energy $(\text{kJ}\,\text{mol}^{-1})$
1	1000
2	2000

OCR examination papers use the solidus as a convention, thus:

Measurement	Ionisation energy / $\text{kJ}\,\text{mol}^{-1}$
1	1000
2	2000

Any numbers appearing in brackets with the units, for example $(10^{-5}\,\text{mol}\,\text{dm}^{-3}\,\text{s}^{-1})$, should be treated in exactly the same way as when preceded by the solidus, $/10^{-5}\,\text{mol}\,\text{dm}^{-3}\,\text{s}^{-1}$.

Telecommunications – an A2 option text

Telecommunications is all that is needed to cover the A2 physics option module of the same name. It is a brand new text which has been written specifically with the new OCR specification in mind. At the end of the book you will find a glossary of terms and answers to both self-assessment questions and end-of-chapter questions.

Bibliography

All the following texts are good and reliable introductions.

Young, Paul (1985), *Electronic Communication Techniques*, Bell & Howell

Green, D. C. (1985), *Radio Systems for Technicians*, Pitman

Langley, Graham (1991), *Telecommunications Primer*, Pitman

Peterson, David (1992), *Audio Video and Data Telecommunications*, McGraw-Hill

Hecht, Jeff (1993), *Understanding Fiber Optics*, Sams Publishing

Green, D. C. (1995), *Data Communication*, Longman

Carne, E. Bryan (1995), *Telecommunications Primer*, Prentice-Hall PTR

Johnson, J. J. & Fletcher, B. D. (1997), *Introductory Radio and Television Electronics*, Macmillan

Couch, Leon W. (1997), *Digital and Analogue Communication Systems*, Prentice-Hall

Gralla, Preston (1999), *How the Internet Works*, QUE

Horowitz, P. and Hill, W. (1989), *The Art of Electronics 2ed*, Cambridge University Press

Brimicombe, M. W. (2000), *Electronics Explained*, Nelson

CHAPTER 1

Historical background

By the end of this chapter you should be able to:

1 understand the need for a *carrier* to be *modulated* in all communication systems;

2 appreciate the importance of the discovery and control of *electricity*;

3 understand the *telegraph* system on land and under water;

4 understand the early *telephone* system;

5 understand the early *radio* system;

6 begin to appreciate the profound effect of modern communications on people's lives.

Introduction

The communication system with which we are most familiar is that of person to person; this system will serve to illustrate the shared characteristics of all communication systems. *Figure 1.1* shows person *A* trying to speak to person *B*. Consider what is required to make this system operate successfully:

- there has to be a **source of information** (*A*'s brain and voice);
- there has to be a **carrier** for this information (the sound wave);
- there has to be a **receiver** for the information (*B*'s ear and brain).

Suppose that, during all the years of his existence, *A* had made the sound 'Ahhh ...', continuously, without ever changing the volume or pausing for breath. If this constant sound were the only sound *A* could make, then *A* could not communicate his thoughts by his voice. That is to say, it would be impossible for *A* to tell *B* anything.

Now suppose that *A* can switch off the sound at will. Thus, *A* can either say 'Ahhh ...' or nothing. This allows *A* and *B* to devise a series of codes to communicate basic information, such as danger, food, good, bad. The point to be noted is that as long as *A* and *B* agree on the codes then it is possible to transmit information as a series of simple grunts. It is conceivable that our ancient ancestors communicated in just such a primitive manner, until they developed the means to vary both the amplitude and the frequency of the 'Ahhh ...' sound.

This example highlights the most fundamental feature of all communication systems: it is impossible to transmit any information unless the carrier is made to vary: i.e. to change or wobble in some way. The change is called **modulation**, and the ways in which this can be done are many and ingenious. Speech is a complex modulation technique, and language is the coding system for information transfer.

Communication by sound, of course, is limited to the range over which someone can shout or bang a drum, and to transfer messages over longer distances other carrier systems were developed.

● **Figure 1.1** Basic communication.

One such carrier system uses ink on paper. What can you read in the following letter?

There is no information in the letter, because the lines are unmodulated; it is only when the pen is made to wobble that the communication system becomes viable.

SAQ 1.1

State and explain what is modulated in documents intended for blind people to read.

There have been many long-distance communication systems invented throughout history; the complexity of the information that can be carried is related to the sophistication of the modulating process. For example, fires on hilltops used light as the carrier with the most elementary modulation technique: 'fire off' or 'fire on'. All the major technological developments in communication, however, have followed the science of electricity and this began only two hundred years ago.

The telegraph system

In 1800, the Italian inventor, Count Alessandro Volta, first showed how to make batteries and produce electric currents. In 1819, the Dutch scientist, Hans Christian Oersted, discovered that electric currents generated magnetic fields and that the strength of the field increased with the strength of the current. In 1825, William Sturgeon used this effect to produce the first **electromagnet**, by winding a wire into a coil around a piece of soft iron. When the wire carried a current, the soft iron became strongly

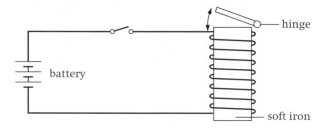

● **Figure 1.2** An electromagnet. When the switch is closed, the current flows and the soft iron core becomes magnetised. In turn magnetism is induced in the hinged lever, which is then attracted to the soft iron core.

magnetised. This strong magnetic field was made to attract and move a hinged lever against a spring, so that the moving lever could be made to perform various functions. For example, it could move a pointer, close or open a switch, move a pen on paper or strike a bell. An electromagnet mechanism is illustrated in *figure 1.2*.

In 1837, Charles Wheatstone and William Cooke invented a **telegraph** system using five electromagnets, each of which could move a different pointer. By energising any two electromagnets at a time, they caused the pointers to select one of 20 letters at a distant location. In this way they were able (albeit very slowly) to transmit written information using a limited alphabet. Their telegraph is shown in *figure 1.3*. From then on, all devices using electromagnets to transfer coded written information were referred to as telegraph systems (the word 'telegraph' comes from the Greek: *tele graphos* means 'far away writing').

Wheatstone's and Cooke's first working telegraph system was set up between two London railway

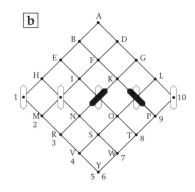

● **Figure 1.3 a** An early form of Cooke's and Wheatstone's telegraph. **b** A five-needle telegraph.

stations, Euston and Camden Town, about 2 km apart. Two years later, in 1839, a second telegraph link was set up between Paddington and Slough railway stations, which were about 30 km apart.

In 1843, Samuel Morse set up a working telegraph system between Washington DC and Baltimore over a distance of about 60 km. In this system, the electromagnet at the receiving end pressed a pen onto moving paper when the switch at the transmitting end was closed. A single wire linking the two cities was suspended from wooden poles that became known as telegraph poles (and, originally, the Earth was used for the return current). The message received consisted of long and short pen marks on the paper, corresponding to long and short pulses of current. It was soon realised, however, that the hammering action of the pen on the paper was generating long and short sounds; these sounds were often easier for the operators to decode, so the moving paper was sometimes discarded. The **Morse code** (*figure 1.4*) became widely used because it minimised transmission times.

SAQ 1.2

Can you think of a reason why Morse gave shorter codes of dots and dashes to some letters than to others?

There is a fundamental problem with the telegraph system when the distance between the transmitter and receiver becomes very great, as the following example will illustrate. Suppose that, in order to energise the electromagnet and move the lever, a minimum current I of 0.5 A is required. Now suppose that the resistance per unit length of the copper wire being used is $10\,\Omega\,km^{-1}$. If the distance between the transmitter and receiver is 1000 km, then the total resistance R of the two cables will be

$$R = 2 \times 10 \times 1000 = 20\,000\,\Omega$$

Thus the battery voltage V required at the transmitting end is given by

$$V = IR = 0.5 \times 20\,000 = 10\,000 \text{ volts!}$$

Such a battery voltage would be extremely dangerous to the operator, and trying to switch it on and off rapidly would probably result in inductive arcing across the switch contacts.

To solve this problem, Morse interrupted the transmission line with regularly spaced electro-magnetic switches so that, when the original transmit switch was closed, a relatively low-voltage battery caused just enough current to energise the first electromagnet a few kilometres away (*figure 1.5*). When the first electromagnet was energised, the switching contacts closed in the second circuit, which also contained a battery; the current flowing in the second circuit energised an electro-magnet a few kilometres farther on. So, when the transmit switch is pressed, the chain of electro-magnets is energised, one after the other, down the line. Thus each electromagnet relays the original signal and, for this reason, such electromagnetic switches were called **relays**.

The telegraph under water

The first submarine cable was laid in 1851, between England and France under the Straits of Dover. This required solving three fundamental problems on cable strength, insulation and conductivity.

- A submarine cable can be placed under very high tension when it is being laid onto or picked up from the sea bed, or if it is struck by a trailing anchor. For this reason, cables were armoured with heavy steel.
- Sea-water is extremely corrosive to metals, so considerable care had to be taken with the insulation: several layers of jute and wax were used. The on/off signal current was carried by a central conductor and the return current was allowed to flow through the sea itself.

A .—.	B —..	C —.—.	D —..
E .	F ..—.	G ——.	H ....
I ..	J .———	K —.—	L .—..
M ——	N —.	O ———	P .——.
Q ..—.	R .—.	S ...	T —
U ..—	V ...—	W .——	X —..—
Y —.——	Z ——..		

● **Figure 1.4** The Morse code; this code of dots and dashes is essentially binary.

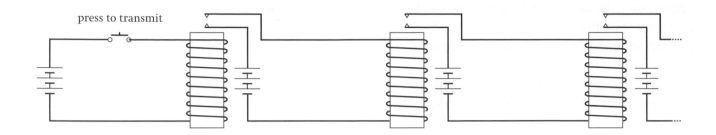

press to transmit

● **Figure 1.5** Relays. As used to maintain the strength of a signal over a long distance.

■ The central conductor had to be thick copper in order to have a very low resistance per unit length, because it was not possible to fit and power relays in a submarine cable. It was also necessary to develop sensitive electromagnets that could be energised by the relatively small currents flowing in such a long cable.

In 1857, two attempts were made to lay a cable across the Atlantic Ocean but both failed. In 1858, a further attempt was made but the system only worked for three weeks until an operator applied 2000 V to the cable and ruined it. Technical and political problems then held up progress for the next eight years.

In 1866, just after the American Civil War, a submarine cable was successfully laid across the Atlantic Ocean. This allowed on/off coded signals to be sent directly between the British Isles and the United States. The first specialised cable-laying ship was launched in 1872 and by 1875 there was an entire network of submarine cables linking many countries of the world (*figure 1.6*). Indeed, as early as 1865, the International Telegraph Union was formed by 20 countries in order that the proposed worldwide communications network would use standardised equipment and operating procedures.

It is interesting to note that on/off currents (i.e. digital signals) were used in telegraph cables under water for almost 100 years, from before the telephone was invented until the latter half of the twentieth century. Although the land-based

● **Figure 1.6** This map shows the underwater cables in operation in 1875.

telephone system was already quite well developed by this time, it was not possible to make a long-distance telephone call under water. Telephony requires repeated amplification of the signal (chapter 5), and long-life, trouble-free amplifiers that could operate for many years in a torpedo tube at the bottom of the sea were not developed until the 1950s.

SAQ 1.3

Suggest why so much effort went into developing and laying cable under water.

The early telephone system

In 1876, Alexander Graham Bell was awarded a patent in the USA for his invention of the **telephone**. This was the first system that successfully transmitted a continuously changing voice signal by means of a continuously changing electric current. A **transducer** (a device that transforms energy from one form to another) was used to convert voice sounds to electric signals and vice versa. The original transducer, which could both transmit and receive, was an electro-magnet made from a coil of fine wire wound around a bar magnet. In front of the coil was a thin iron diaphragm, fixed around its edge so that it could move in and out like a drum skin. If the coil carried a varying current, the diaphragm was pushed and pulled by the rapidly varying magnetic field from the electromagnet and so generated sound. If, however, sound waves impinged on the diaphragm then it vibrated with the sound waves and caused the magnetic flux to vary, so that a small e.m.f. was induced in the coil. A diagram of Bell's transducer is shown in *figure 1.7*, and *figure 1.8* shows a simple telephone system using two such transducers.

The carrier of information in this telephone system was the set of randomly moving free electrons in the circuit. A small alternating **drift velocity** – i.e. an alternating current – modulated this random motion when a person spoke into the microphone. There was no battery in the circuit, thus the small a.c. current produced only faint sounds in the receiver. Furthermore, there was no

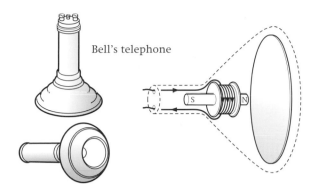

Bell's telephone

● **Figure 1.7** Bell's telephone.

● **Figure 1.8** A basic telephone circuit.

means of signalling to a potential user that a caller wished to speak.

It must be remembered that no electronic amplifiers existed at this time (electronics, as we know it today, did not begin until 1907 when Lee deForest invented the triode valve) but, even so, several people sought to improve Bell's system by making the current and consequently the sound stronger.

In 1877, Thomas Alva Edison developed a carbon microphone which, when a direct current was passed through it, behaved like a **sound-dependent resistor**. By adding a battery to the circuit, the carbon microphone caused a larger variation in current than Bell's original transducer, so louder sounds were heard in the receiver. The resulting system is shown in *figure 1.9* overleaf.

SAQ 1.4

Compare the operation of a string telephone (a taut string) with the electrical one shown in *figure 1.7*.

The early radio system

In 1867, James Clerk Maxwell translated Michael Faraday's many experiments on electricity and magnetism (together with the results of Coulomb,

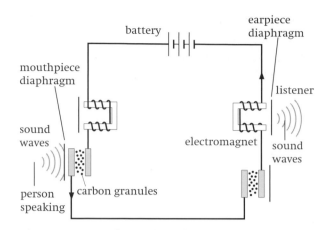

● **Figure 1.9** A carbon-microphone telephone.

Ampère and others) into a mathematical theory that predicted the existence of electromagnetic waves. In 1887, seven years after Maxwell's death, Heinrich Hertz became the first person to generate and detect these waves, in the area of the electromagnetic spectrum to which we now refer as **radio waves**. He produced them from an *induction coil* powered by a low-voltage battery. The input circuit of an induction coil operates in a similar manner to an electric bell: an energised electromagnet repeatedly makes and breaks its own current and so causes large variations in the flux of its magnetic core. This flux links a secondary coil with many turns, and so at each flux change a high voltage is created across the output terminals of the secondary. Thus the output circuit is essentially the secondary of a step-up transformer generating several thousand volts. The rapidly varying high voltage caused repeated sparks across an air gap (*figure 1.10*).

The rapidly varying current in the induction-coil sparks generated radio waves, and Hertz used a broken hoop as an aerial to detect these radio waves at a distance. The waves revealed their presence by causing tiny sparks to jump across the air gap in the hoop. In this way, Hertz was able to show that the radiation from the transmitter genuinely had the wave properties Maxwell had predicted. His loop aerial, however, was not sufficiently sensitive to detect the new radio waves at greater distances. He died at a young age and thus never found out whether radio waves could be made to travel any significant distance.

Guglielmo Marconi was only 20 years old when he first read of Hertz's discovery of electromagnetic waves. The young Italian repeated and developed these experiments and was soon demonstrating radio-wave communication over 10 metres in his father's estate in Bologna. His early system used a sparking induction coil as a transmitter but a glass tube of metal filings as a receiver. The glass tube was called a **coherer** because the metal filings cohered, or stuck together, when the radio waves reached the receiver. The cohered filings effectively closed a circuit containing a battery and bell, so that the bell was rung without any connecting wires between the transmitter and receiver. This became known as **wireless** transmission. A diagram of Marconi's apparatus is shown in *figure 1.11*.

By 1895, Marconi had so improved his apparatus that he was able to transmit and detect a radio signal beyond the range of sight. His own government, however, showed little interest in his work and as a result he moved to England, where he received support from the Post Office.

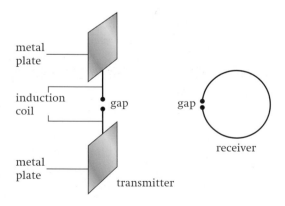

● **Figure 1.10** A diagrammatic form of Hertz's original apparatus for transmitting and detecting a radio wave.

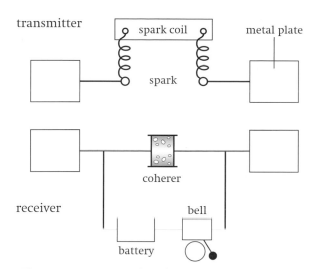

● **Figure 1.11** Marconi's wireless apparatus.

In 1897, Marconi was awarded his first patent, after which he set up the Wireless and Telegraph Signal Company. He set out to prove that on/off radio waves could carry coded information over long distances (*figure 1.12*), despite having been told by many scientists and engineers that his efforts would come to nothing. They believed the curvature of the Earth would place a limit on the transmission distance of about 100 kilometres.

In 1901, Marconi performed the demonstration which was to make him famous. In Poldhu in Cornwall, his company built a transmitter that was a hundred times more powerful than any-thing they had used before and set up an aerial made up from two poles from which wires spread out like a fan. At Signal Hill in Newfoundland,

● **Figure 1.12** Marconi (right) operating his radio link between England and France, 1899.

across the Atlantic, Marconi himself suspended an aerial from a kite flying at a height of over 100 metres. The kite stayed up long enough for the redoubtable experimenter to detect transmission of the Morse-coded letter 'S' from England, over 3000 km away.

One common feature of these early electrical methods, the telegraph, the telephone and wireless telegraphy, is that they were designed to be **point-to-point** systems of communication. That is to say, they were designed for a single transmitter and a single receiver. However, in 1906, Reginald Fessenden became the first person to **broadcast** an analogue signal using radio waves. He transmitted from Brant Rock, near Boston, on the eastern seaboard of the United States (see chapter 3). His radio waves were crudely amplitude modulated to broadcast a violin solo and picked up by many wireless telegraph operators who happened to have their headphones on at the time. These operators became the first people in history to hear music carried by radio waves.

Impact of modern communications

Having discovered how to produce and control electric currents, successive generations of scientists and engineers have made the processes of communicating over longer and longer distances faster and faster, with more and more information being carried for lower and lower prices. This has resulted in many dramatic changes to the ways in which people now expect to live their lives when compared with their ancestors of only a few generations ago.

World news, for example, is now broadcast (by radio or television) as and where it happens, so that any listener or viewer can be kept up to date with current affairs. World entertainment can similarly be broadcast, and this allows exposure of one culture to another. In the developed world, the use of the telephone has become so wide-spread that instant person-to-person communication is often taken for granted. Indeed, the ease with which communication can be established using the telephone has resulted in a dramatic decline in the use of the personal letter. Furthermore, the mobile phone has allowed instant communication from almost any locality and this has provided not only business potential but also a greater sense of security for its users. The relatively recent popularisation of the Internet has caused huge numbers of businesses to appear whose commercial operations provide employment to some and services to a great many.

Aspects of the impact of modern communications are mentioned throughout the book; see for example pages 66, 75, 80, 90 and 101.

SUMMARY

◆ A carrier is needed to transfer information.

◆ The carrier must be modulated in some way by the information.

◆ Electrically driven communication systems have been around for nearly two centuries.

◆ The telegraph system used Morse-coded pulses of current.

◆ The telegraph under water was more difficult to establish than on land.

◆ The early telephone system used a transducer and a varying current.

◆ The early radio system used Morse-coded bursts of electromagnetic waves.

Questions

1   Explain why, although it has a varying voltage, mains electricity does not communicate information.

2   The complete works of William Shakespeare fill a 1200-page book with an average of about 1000 words per page. Estimate the length of time it would take a Guide to communicate the entire volume using semaphore. (This is a system where two flags can be moved by the hands to any one of 28 positions (*figure 1.13*).)

3   In Morse's original telegraph, the Earth was used for the return current. Suggest why it was set up in this way.

4   By focussing on connections, distance of transmission and potential customers, explain why the original telephone system appeared to have a very limited future.

5   Explain the difference between point-to-point communication and broadcasting.

● **Figure 1.13** The semaphore code. Each letter corresponds to a position of the two flags.

CHAPTER 2

Characteristics of waveforms and information

By the end of this chapter you should be able to:

1 determine the *amplitude* and *frequency* of a signal from a suitable graph;

2 understand that a signal waveform can be represented in time or frequency;

3 recall that any waveform can be resolved into or synthesised from sinusoidal components;

4 understand the *bandwidth* of a signal;

5 appreciate the differences in bandwidth between audio and video information;

6 describe an *analogue* signal in terms of continuous variation between two limits;

7 describe a *digital* signal as one having two states only;

8 represent an analogue and a digital signal graphically;

9 understand the use of *analogue-to-digital* and *digital-to-analogue* converters;

10 understand the significance of *word-length* for the quality of the output signal.

Oscillations

Telecommunications makes use of physical quantities which can be made to wobble, or **oscillate**. Examples of such quantities are the displacement of air molecules in a sound wave, the light intensity in an optic fibre, the current in a cable and the electric and magnetic fields in an electromagnetic wave. Each of these oscillating quantities, which we can call x, exhibits **wave motion**; the simplest form of wave motion can be represented by the two sinusoidal graphs shown in *figure 2.1* overleaf.

In *figure 2.1a* we see x as a function of distance at some instant in time (rather like a snapshot of the wave). We can observe the **wavelength** λ as the distance between two successive points with the same **phase**. In *figure 2.1b*, we see how the value of x at a particular distance varies with time; think of a cork going up and down on a pond as ripples pass. From this graph we can observe the **time period** T (the

time taken for one oscillation, i.e. peak to trough and back to peak). The time period T allows us to calculate the **frequency** f of the oscillation:

$$f = \frac{1}{T}$$

Imagine that as a wave reaches it, the cork starts to oscillate. Each time it does so, the wave moves forward by λ. If the frequency is f then the wave will move forward by a distance $f\lambda$ each second – but this must be its **speed** v. Thus λ and f are related to the v of the wave by

$$v = f\lambda$$

The equation describing the oscillating quantity x (e.g. displacement, intensity, current, voltage, electric field) in *figure 2.1b* is then

$$x = A \sin \omega t$$

where ω is known as the **angular frequency** ($\omega = 2\pi f$) and A is the amplitude of the oscillation.

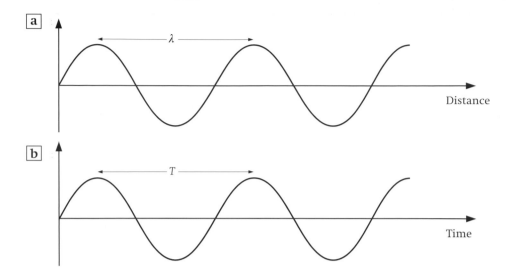

● **Figure 2.1** How the amplitude of a simple waveform varies **a** with distance and **b** with time.

Analysing waveforms

Jean Baptiste Fourier was the mathematician who first explained that a waveform of any shape can be made up from a series of sine waves having different frequencies; this is **Fourier analysis**. When these sine waves are added together in the correct proportions, the sum is the original waveform. The series of sine waves begins with the **fundamental**, or **first harmonic**, which has the same frequency f as the original waveform. The series continues with the **second harmonic**, of frequency $2f$, the **third harmonic**, of frequency $3f$ and so on. The amplitudes of the various harmonics depend on the shape of the original waveform. Thus, the simplest waveform has only a fundamental and no other harmonics: this is a pure sine wave. Such a wave in sound is often referred to as a **pure tone**.

A classic example of waveform analysis is the search for the components of a perfect square wave. This can be shown to be made up from a fundamental added to an infinite number of odd harmonics of ever decreasing amplitude. The expression for such a square wave is

$$x = A \sin \omega t + \frac{A}{3} \sin 3\omega t + \frac{A}{5} \sin 5\omega t + \cdots$$

In *figure 2.2* the fundamental, third, fifth and seventh harmonics are drawn separately and then added together. The sum clearly shows the emerging square wave.

The perfect square waveform x (*figure 2.3a*) can be described fully by listing the angular frequencies ω present in the series, together with their amplitudes A, $A/3$, $A/5$ and so on. When this information is displayed as a graph, we obtain *figure 2.3b*. In practice, the frequency, $f = \omega/2\pi$, is often used instead of ω, giving the graph shown in *figure 2.3c*.

So, the plotting of any waveform x as a function of frequency displays the amplitudes and distribution of harmonics in the waveform. This graph is known as the **spectrum** of the waveform. We can see that the spectrum of a pure sine wave is simply a straight line (i.e. it is composed of only one frequency) while the spectrum of a perfect square wave consists of an infinite number of ever decreasing lines (*figure 2.3c*).

SAQ 2.1

A waveform is analysed and is found to contain two frequencies of the same amplitude. One frequency is 500 Hz and the other is 1000 Hz. Draw the waveform as a function of time and also as a function of frequency.

Bandwidth

In telecommunications, all signals have waveforms that can be analysed, as discussed above, for their frequency content. This analysis allows the signal's bandwidth to be determined.

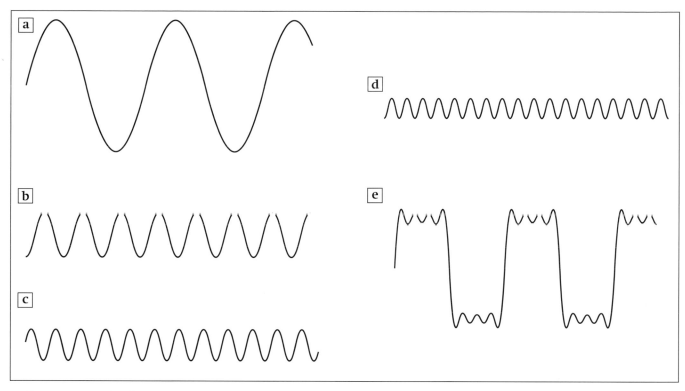

● **Figure 2.2 a** The fundamental; **b** third harmonic (three times the fundamental frequency); **c** fifth harmonic; **d** seventh harmonic. **e** The fundamental plus the third, fifth and seventh harmonics are added in the proportions shown by their amplitudes to give an emerging square wave.

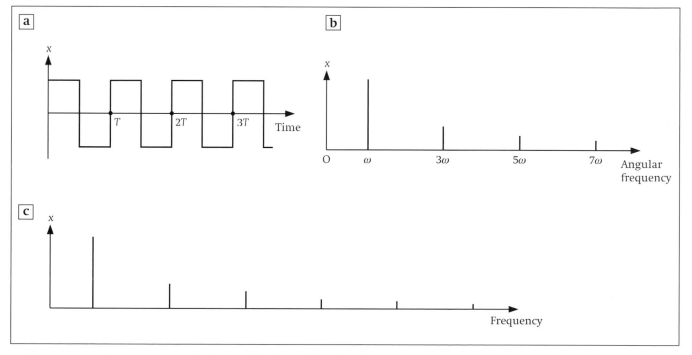

● **Figure 2.3 a** A square wave; **b** the amplitudes of its first four harmonics plotted against angular frequency ω; **c** the amplitudes of its first six harmonics plotted against frequency f.

The **bandwidth** of a signal is the range of frequencies required to make up the signal. That is, the bandwidth equals the highest-frequency component minus the lowest-frequency component.

Thus we see that the bandwidth of a pure sine wave is zero, because it occupies only one frequency. However, the bandwidth of a perfect square wave is infinite, because to represent a square wave using sine waves we need an infinite range of sine waves. Now we will consider the band-widths required for audio and video information.

Audio information

Speech

We speak by causing our vocal chords to vibrate in such a way that the surrounding air molecules are alternately compressed and rarefied, causing a sound wave to be produced. The sound is made up of vowels and consonants. *Figure 2.4* shows the displacements of an air molecule for a simplified vowel sound and for a simplified consonant sound.

A typical voice might produce a sound power of about 15 μW but it is not evenly distributed over the audio frequency range. When the voice is analysed for its frequency content then we obtain spectra like those shown in *figure 2.5*. Note that the process of speaking generates not just one or two but a continuous range of frequencies of waves with constantly changing amplitudes.

Although the typical speaking voice generates frequencies from about 100 Hz to about 10 kHz, it is not necessary to transmit such a large range in a telephone system. In fact, to keep costs down,

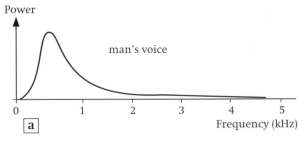

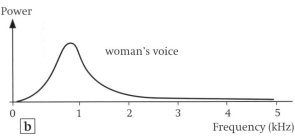

● **Figure 2.5** Typical spectra of **a** a man's voice; **b** a woman's voice.

the range of frequencies transmitted is kept as narrow as possible. There is little power from a voice above 2 kHz, so you might think this frequency would usefully serve as an upper limit. However, most people find speech to be unintelligible with a 2 kHz limit, because 's' and 't' sounds are generated by frequencies higher than this. Consequently, the public telephone network uses a bandwidth of 3.1 kHz in the range 300 Hz to 3.4 kHz, because within this range we are mostly able to recognise a caller's voice.

Music

Our ears are sensitive to a much greater range of frequencies than those transmitted by a normal telephone. In general, music produced from a variety of instruments will cover a range from about 20 Hz to about 20 kHz. However, to keep costs down, broadcasters of music restrict the range actually transmitted to suit the band-width of the channel being used for broadcasting. The BBC, for example, has two standards: **high fidelity**, (20 Hz to 15 kHz) used on very high frequency (VHF) radio, and **low fidelity**, (100 Hz to 3.5 kHz)

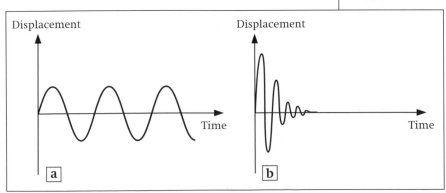

● **Figure 2.4** Waveforms **a** for a vowel sound; **b** for a consonant.

used on long-wave (LW) and medium-wave (MW) radio.

If you transmit music through a telephone network designed only for speech, it will be of very low fidelity indeed.

Video information

Television

The basic principles of television follow those of the cinema where a series of still pictures is projected, one after the other, so that the brain perceives motion. The sense of motion occurs because of persistence of vision in the eye. In Europe, the projection rate is 25 pictures per second.

A monochrome (i.e. black and white) TV picture is built up as a series of parallel lines. Each line is produced by a beam of electrons sweeping across the screen from left to right. The electron beam current is varied by the incoming signal so as to cause varying degrees of brightness on the phosphor on the inside of the screen.

To find the relation between the bandwidth needed for transmission of a TV picture and the characteristics of the screen, we adopt the following approach.

The screen is characterised by its resolution, i.e. the degree of detail it can display. The vertical resolution is governed by the number of horizontal lines used. For national TV broadcast in Europe, the number of scanning lines is chosen to be 625, but only 575 of these are actually used for drawing the picture; the remaining 50 are used for synchronisation pulses and teletext. The aspect ratio (i.e. the width of the screen divided by the height of the screen) of the standard TV is $4:3$. To obtain the same resolution horizontally as vertically, there have to be $\frac{4}{3} \times 575$ phosphor points per line. The highest signal frequency with which the screen can cope will correspond to the most detailed picture that the electron beam can draw: alternate white (current on) and black (current off) dots along each row. Such a picture would look like a series of striated vertical bars (*figure 2.6*).

To draw each line, the signal has to switch on and off $(\frac{4}{3} \times 575)/2$ times. To draw the whole array, this procedure has to be repeated 575 times. If all

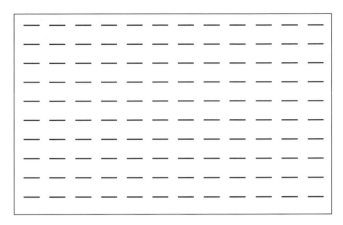

● **Figure 2.6** The most detailed possible television picture is a series of horizontal bars.

this happens in one second, the required switching frequency is $575 \times (\frac{4}{3} \times 575)/2$ Hz. If it is to happen 25 times a second then the required switching frequency is

$$25 \times 575 \times \tfrac{4}{3} \times 575/2 \text{ Hz} = 5.5 \text{ MHz.}$$

This is the highest allowable frequency at which the video signal can switch the electron gun on and off. The lowest video frequency is essentially d.c. (i.e. 0 Hz) and this corresponds to a blank picture. Hence the bandwidth required is 5.5 MHz.

SAQ 2.2

A security camera in a bank takes two pictures every second. Each picture is composed of 300 lines with 400 phosphor points per line. Calculate the picture bandwidth.

Analogue and digital signals

The information carried in modern telecommunication systems may be broadly categorised as **audio**, **video** or **data**. This information enters the system through a transducer and generates a signal voltage. This voltage may be termed the **information signal**; it will be either **analogue** or **digital**.

An **analogue** signal is one which varies in time in an *analogous* manner to the physical property which generated it. These signals are continuous in time and can have any value between two limits (*figure 2.7a*). An example of an analogue signal is the voltage generated by a microphone, as this is proportional to the displacement–time graph of the molecules of air in front of it.

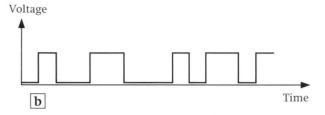

• **Figure 2.7 a** Analogue signal; **b** digital signal.

A **digital** signal does not vary continuously with time; it can have only two values, say 1 or 0 (*figure 2.7b*). It is essentially a coded representation of the original information. We indicate below how a digital signal is obtained from an analogue signal. An example of a digital signal is the stream of high and low voltages produced from a digitised telephone call. This will be discussed in chapter 9.

SAQ 2.3

A potential divider circuit is composed of a thermistor (a device whose resistance changes markedly with temperature) and a resistor connected in series across a power supply. State and explain whether the p.d. across the thermistor will be an analogue or a digital signal.

Decimal to binary equals digital

In our familiar **decimal** system, we have ten symbols (0 to 9) to represent numbers. For example, if we have six items then we write 6, but if we have ten items then we have run out of symbols and must start a new column by writing 10. Each time we run out of symbols, we start a new column. For example, one greater than ninety-nine is written as 100.

Any number written using the decimal system is an array of digits corresponding to powers of

ten. For example, the number two thousand, three hundred and fifty-eight can be written as

$$2358 = 2 \times 10^3 + 3 \times 10^2 + 5 \times 10^1 + 8 \times 10^0$$

The left-hand digit, here 2, is the most significant digit and the right-hand digit, here 8, is the least significant digit.

In the **binary** system, we have only two symbols, 0 and 1, but otherwise we count in exactly the same way as in the decimal system. Thus if we have one item we write 1, but if we have two items then we have run out of symbols and must start a new column by writing 10. 'Three' is written 11, and one greater than three is written 100. Thus any number written using the binary system is an array of **binary digits** representing multiples of powers of two. Each binary digit is called a **bit**.

For example, forty-three items would be written as 101011 since

$$forty\text{-}three = 1 \times 2^5 + 0 \times 2^4 + 1 \times 2^3 + 0 \times 2^2 + 1 \times 2^1 + 1 \times 2^0$$

The left-hand 1 is the most significant bit and the right-hand 1 is the least significant bit.

It can be seen that numbers written in the binary system, such as 101011, are in **digital** form.

SAQ 2.4

a Write down the binary equivalent of the decimal number 49.

b Write down the decimal equivalent of the binary number 100110.

Analogue to digital

Using a modern integrated circuit (IC), it is now easy to convert an analogue signal into a digital signal. This IC is described as an **analogue-to-digital converter** (ADC). The digital signal can be converted back into the corresponding analogue signal using a **digital-to-analogue** converter (DAC).

In order to gain some understanding of the processes involved in these conversions, consider the diagram of *figure 2.8a*. A potentiometer (a variable resistor) is connected across a 16 volt power

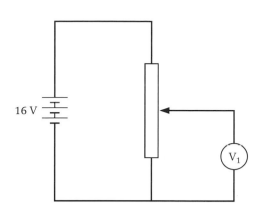
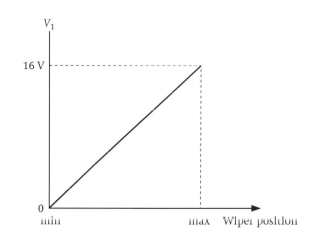

● **Figure 2.8 a** A generalised potentiometer circuit; **b** a graph to show how voltage varies with wiper position.

supply, so that the wiper (the movable contact) can be set to provide any voltage between 0 V and 16 V. The wiper is connected to a moving coil analogue voltmeter, which registers a voltage V_1.

The wiper voltage is an analogue signal because it is proportional to the physical position of the wiper, and the meter is termed an analogue meter because the angle turned by the pointer is proportional to the wiper voltage. *Figure 2.8* also shows a graph of the voltmeter reading as a function of the position of the wiper. It is a straight line and indicates that the meter voltage V_1 can take any value between 0 V and 16 V.

Now consider the diagram shown in *figure 2.9*, where the wiper is connected to the input of a **two-bit** ADC. The two-bit output of the ADC is connected to the input of a two-bit DAC. The output of the DAC is connected to an analogue moving coil

voltmeter like that used in *figure 2.8*. In this way, we are generating an analogue signal, converting it to a digital signal, transmitting the digital signal and then converting it back to analogue.

Word length

Because the ADC is only two-bit, there can only be $2^2 = 4$ possible outputs or **words** that it can produce. These are

0–4 V	0 0
4–8 V	1 0
8–12 V	0 1
12–16 V	1 1

The **word-length** equals the number of bits in the word; here the word-length is two.

If the matched DAC is also two-bit, then it can only accept one of the above four input combinations and thus it can only have four possible output values between 0 V and 16 V (i.e. the DAC output could be 0, 4, 8 or 12 V).

Figure 2.10 gives the readings on the two voltmeters V_1 and V_2 as the wiper is moved from minimum to maximum. These two graphs show the difference between the pure analogue signal V_1 (which can have any value) and the recovered analogue signal V_2 (which can only have four distinct values). The output of the DAC is said to be **quantised**, and in this case it would have a (relatively huge) **quantisation error**, the difference

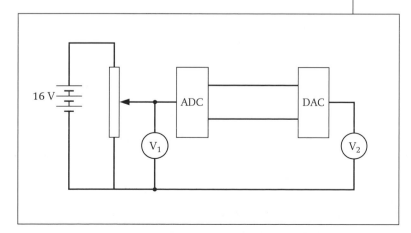

● **Figure 2.9** A potentiometer circuit feeding into a two-bit ADC.

between adjacent readings, of about 4 V.

Now consider the circuit of *figure 2.11*. Here the ADC has been replaced by a three-bit converter, so there are now $2^3 = 8$ possible outputs (words) it can produce.

These are

0–2 V	0 0 0
2–4 V	1 0 0
4–6 V	0 1 0
6–8 V	1 1 0
8–10 V	0 0 1
10–12 V	1 0 1
12–14 V	0 1 1
14–16 V	1 1 1

If the matched DAC is also three-bit, then it can accept any of the above eight input combinations and so produce eight possible output values between 0 V and 16 V, i.e. the DAC output could be 0, 2, 4, 6, 8, 10, 12 or 14 V.

Figure 2.12 gives the readings on the two voltmeters V_1 and V_2 as the wiper is moved from minimum to maximum. This figure shows that the recovered analogue signal V_2 is still quantised but looks more like the original analogue input, with a reduced quantisation error. So you can see that the greater is the bit number (i.e. word-length) of the ADC and matching DAC, the greater is the number of possible output combinations and thus the smaller are the quantisation steps in the recovered signal.

For example, if the ADC and DAC are 12-bit converters (quite normal in today's electronics) then the number of possible outputs of the ADC is 2^{12} and so the

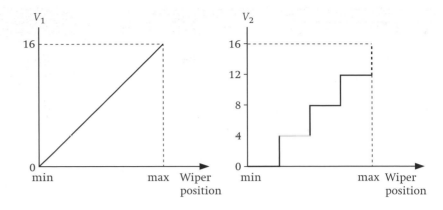

● **Figure 2.10** V_1 and V_2 with a two-bit ADC output.

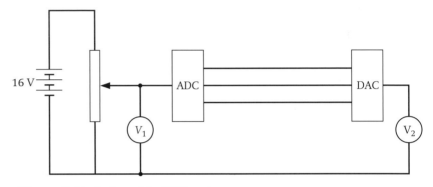

● **Figure 2.11** A three-bit ADC system.

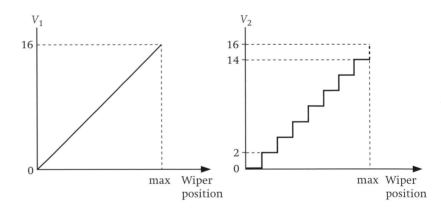

● **Figure 2.12** V_1 and V_2 with a three-bit output.

steps in the output voltage would be of height $16\,V/2^{12} = 16/4096 \approx 4\,mV$. The difference between V_1 and V_2 would hardly be noticeable. Thus the word-length is very important in determining the quality of the final output in digital transmission.

SUMMARY

◆ A wave is characterised by its wavelength λ, frequency f and amplitude A.

◆ Wave speed is the product of frequency and wavelength, $v = f\lambda$.

◆ The simplest form of oscillation is a sinusoidal function of time: $x = A \sin \omega t$.

◆ Any waveform is made up of a fundamental and appropriate harmonics.

◆ The bandwidth of a waveform or signal is the range of frequencies making up the signal.

◆ Audio transmission requires a bandwidth of the order of kHz.

◆ Broadcast TV requires a bandwidth of the order of MHz.

◆ An analogue signal is a continuous representation of a physical property.

◆ A digital signal is a coded series of 1s and 0s.

◆ Digitising analogue signals results in quantisation errors.

◆ Quantisation can be reduced by increasing the number of bits on the ADC and DAC.

Questions

1 Sound travels at standard temperature and pressure with a velocity of $330 \, \mathrm{m \, s^{-1}}$. Calculate the wavelength of the pure tone A (440 Hz).

2 Electromagnetic waves travel in a vacuum with velocity $3 \times 10^8 \, \mathrm{m \, s^{-1}}$. Calculate the frequency of a 6 cm microwave.

3 A person with a hearing disorder can detect only sounds between 400 Hz and 8.4 kHz. Calculate the person's audible bandwidth.

4 Calculate the number of output states possible for an eight-bit ADC.

5 An analogue signal that can vary over the range 0 V to +9 V is digitised by a 16-bit ADC and then reconstructed by a 16-bit DAC. Estimate the size of the quantisation error in the reconstructed signal.

CHAPTER 3

Amplitude modulation and frequency modulation

By the end of this chapter you should be able to:

1 understand that the *baseband* of a signal is the range of frequencies present;

2 understand the term *modulation* and distinguish between amplitude modulation (AM) and frequency modulation (FM);

3 recall that a *carrier wave*, amplitude modulated by a single audio frequency, is equivalent to the carrier-wave frequency together with two sideband frequencies;

4 understand that AM and FM essentially shift the baseband to a higher frequency;

5 demonstrate an awareness of the relative advantages of FM and AM transmissions.

Carriers and baseband

In chapter 1 we saw that an unmodulated carrier wave cannot communicate any information, so that modulation is fundamental to the communication process. The transmission is composed of two parts:

■ the **information signal** (audio, video or data), which is usually changing all the time and can be highly complex;

■ the **carrier wave** (often a radio wave, light wave or a.c. current), which is the means of sending the information.

As we saw in chapter 1, modulation is the process by which some property of the carrier wave (e.g. its amplitude, frequency or phase) is modified by the information. In telecommunications, the range of frequencies in the information signal, for which we have already met the term 'bandwidth', is often referred to as the **baseband**. As we shall see, the processes of amplitude or frequency modulation essentially shift the baseband to a higher frequency range.

Amplitude modulation

In amplitude modulation (AM), the instantaneous value of the information signal (*figure 3.1a*) controls the amplitude of the carrier wave (*figures 3.1b, c*). In this way, the **envelope** (*figure 3.1c*) of the carrier assumes the shape of the information signal.

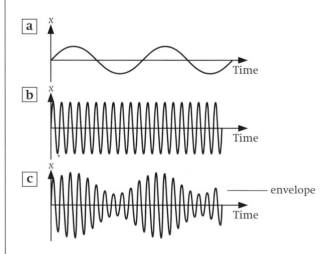

● **Figure 3.1 a** Pure-tone information signal; **b** unmodulated carrier; **c** amplitude-modulated carrier.

Equation for an AM wave

A sinusoidal carrier wave has frequency f_c (angular frequency $\omega_c = 2\pi f_c$), and amplitude A_c. It is described by

$$x_c = A_c \sin \omega_c t$$

The simplest form of *information* signal is also a pure sine wave, with a frequency f_i, say (angular frequency $\omega_i = 2\pi f_i$), and amplitude A_i. It is described by

$$x_i = A_i \sin \omega_i t$$

When the carrier is amplitude modulated, the resulting wave is governed by the equation

$$x_{AM} = (A_c + A_i \sin \omega_i t) \sin \omega_c t$$

Note that the amplitude of the modulated carrier sine function increases and decreases above and below the carrier amplitude A_c by the instantaneous value of the information signal, the second term within the parentheses.

The equation for x_{AM} can be expanded by removing the brackets and applying basic trigonometric identities:

$$x_{AM} = A_c \sin \omega_c t + \tfrac{1}{2} A_i [\cos(\omega_c - \omega_i)t - \cos(\omega_c + \omega_i)t]$$

The first term represents the carrier wave, the second the lower side frequency and the third the upper side frequency.

When the amplitude modulated carrier waveform of *figure 3.1c* is analysed, it is found to be composed of three different components:

- the original carrier wave of frequency f_c and original amplitude A_c;
- a wave of frequency $f_c - f_i$, the **lower side frequency**, and of amplitude $A_i/2$;
- a wave of frequency $f_c + f_i$, the **upper side frequency**, and of amplitude $A_i/2$.

Note that:

- the original information frequency f_i has disappeared;
- the maximum amplitude of the AM carrier is $A_c + A_i$;
- the minimum amplitude of the AM carrier is $A_c - A_i$;
- the carrier frequency f_c must be greater than the information frequency f_i;
- the carrier amplitude A_c must be greater than the information amplitude A_i.

Figure 3.2 shows the spectrum of the AM carrier of *figure 3.1*, i.e. the amplitude of the waveform plotted as a function of frequency (see chapter 2).

It can be seen that the bandwidth of the resulting AM signal is $2f_i$.

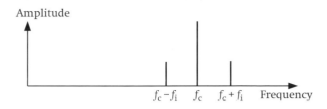

- **Figure 3.2** The graph shows the amplitude of each frequency component of the modulated wave shown in *figure 3.1c*.

Of course, the information signal is very unlikely to be a pure sine wave (i.e. a pure tone) of constant frequency and amplitude. Real signals (whether audio or video) will be composed of a range of frequencies covering a baseband. The amplitudes of the individual frequencies in the baseband will be constantly fluctuating, so any attempt to draw them would produce a fuzzy picture. An example of a low-fidelity music-signal baseband is shown in *figure 3.3*. Thus, if the sinusoidal carrier is amplitude modulated not with a pure tone but with information covering a baseband from $f_{i\,min}$ to $f_{i\,max}$, the spectrum shown in *figure 3.4*, overleaf, is the result. Note that:

- the spectrum is composed of the carrier and the upper and lower sidebands;
- the carrier component is unchanged;
- the information is in the sidebands and not in the carrier;
- the information is duplicated in the two sidebands.

> **The bandwidth required for an AM waveform is twice the maximum frequency in the information.**

- **Figure 3.3** Low-fidelity music baseband.

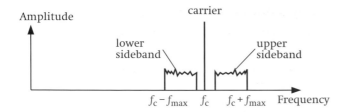

● **Figure 3.4** The bandwidth extends from $f_c - f_{max}$ to $f_c + f_{max}$, where f_{max} is the maximum information frequency. Hence the bandwidth is $2f_{max}$.

The signal represented by *figure 3.4* is known as **double-sideband amplitude modulation** (DSB-AM) and it is a relatively inefficient process. At best, when the carrier is subject to 100% modulation (i.e. $A_i = A_c$), half the transmitted power is in the sinusoidal carrier, where there is no information, and the other half is shared equally between the two sidebands (which contain the same information). Thus, at best, the useful information is contained in only one quarter of the transmitted power.

It is possible to make the process more efficient by eliminating the carrier and transmitting only the two sidebands. This would be called a **double-sideband suppressed-carrier** transmission. The bandwidth, however, remains unchanged.

The most efficient form of AM transmission is to filter out the carrier and one of the sidebands as well. This type of transmission would be termed **single-sideband suppressed-carrier**; not only is it more efficient in terms of power but it also halves the bandwidth required.

You might suppose that single-sideband suppressed-carrier would be the only form of AM in use, but this is not the case; although it is the most efficient it is also the most problematic to demodulate. Single-sideband receivers are consequently more complicated and more expensive than those for DSB-AM.

Information transmitted using AM

Radio
National broadcasts on the long-wave and medium-wave radio networks have always used DSB-AM, because receivers are relatively simple and cheap and thus the population is encouraged to buy and use them.

TV
The luminance (brightness) information for terrestrial television is broadcast using a carrier with one full sideband and a small part of the other sideband. This process is called **vestigial-sideband AM** transmission.

Telephone and radio amateurs
Some of the early mobile-phone systems used, and radio amateurs still use, single-sideband AM because this maximises the use of the available bandwidth. It also has the interesting property that when the information signal drops to zero (i.e. during the silences in conversation) there is no transmitted power at all.

SAQ 3.1
A 100 kHz carrier is amplitude modulated by a 10 kHz square wave. The carrier has an amplitude of 20 V and the square wave has an amplitude of 5 V. Draw a graph of 20 carrier cycles of the resulting AM signal, labelling important points on the voltage and time axes.

Frequency modulation
In frequency modulation (FM), the instantaneous value of the information signal (*figure 3.5a*) controls the frequency of the carrier wave (*figures 3.5b, c*): as the information signal increases, the frequency of the carrier increases, and as the information signal decreases, the frequency of the carrier decreases.

The frequency f_i of the information signal controls the rate at which the carrier frequency increases and decreases. As for AM, f_i must be less than f_c. The amplitude of the carrier remains constant throughout this process.

When the information voltage reaches its peak, the change in carrier frequency will have reached a maximum. This maximum change in frequency of the carrier from its base value f_c is called the **frequency deviation** Δf_c and this sets the dynamic range (i.e. the voltage range) of the transmission.

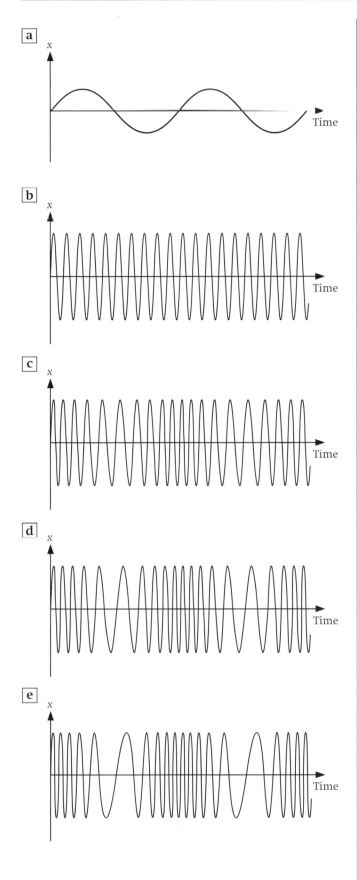

● **Figure 3.5 a** Pure-tone information signal;
b unmodulated carrier; **c** frequency-modulated
(FM) carrier, $m = 3$; **d** FM carrier, $m = 5$; **e** FM
carrier, $m = 7$.

The **dynamic range** is the ratio of the largest and smallest analogue information signals that can be transmitted.

Worked example

A 500 kHz sinusoidal carrier of amplitude 10 V is frequency modulated by a 2 kHz sinusoidal information signal of amplitude 2 V. The behaviour of the carrier is governed by the frequency deviation per volt and this value is 20 kHz per volt. Describe how the resulting FM signal changes with time. Describe how the resulting FM signal will change if the information signal amplitude becomes 3 V.

Solution: The resulting FM carrier will change in frequency (in kHz) from 500 to 540 to 500 to 460 and back to 500 and repeat this cycle 2000 times per second. This is because the frequency deviation $\Delta f_c = 2 \times 20 = 40$ kHz. Throughout, the carrier amplitude will remain steady at 10 V.

If the information signal amplitude becomes 3 V, the carrier frequency will change from 500 to 560 to 500 to 440 and back to 500, again 2000 times per second. This time, the frequency deviation becomes $\Delta f_c = 3 \times 20 = 60$ kHz. As before, the carrier amplitude will remain steady at 10 V.

Modulation index

All FM transmissions are governed by a *modulation index m*, which effectively controls the dynamic range of the information being carried: m is the ratio of the frequency deviation to the maximum information frequency,

$$m = \Delta f_c / f_i$$

Equation for an FM waveform

A sinusoidal carrier of some physical property x is described by

$$x_c = A_c \sin \omega_c t$$

The simplest form of information signal is another pure sine wave, described by

$$x_i = A_i \sin \omega_i t$$

When the carrier is frequency modulated, it is governed by the equation

$$x_{FM} = A_c \sin(\omega_c t + m \sin \omega_i t)$$

where m is known as the **modulation index** and is defined by the equation

$$m = \Delta f_c / f_i$$

Figures 3.5a, b show the information signal and carrier signal for $f_c = 10f_i$. The graphs in figures 3.5c, d, e show how the FM carrier waveform changes for three different values of modulation index. For example, in figure 3.5c, the modulation index m equals 3, corresponding to a frequency deviation Δf_c equal to $3f_i$. Thus the carrier frequency ranges from $10f_i$ to $13f_i$ to $10f_i$ to $7f_i$.

FM spectra

When the amplitudes of the frequency components of an FM waveform are plotted as a function of frequency, the resulting graph (or spectrum) is much more complicated than the equivalent AM spectrum (one carrier + two sidebands). Theoretically, an FM spectrum has an infinite number of sidebands, spaced at multiples of f_i above and below the carrier frequency f_c. However, the size and significance of these sidebands is very dependent on the modulation index m. (Sidebands below 1% of the carrier can be ignored.)

If $m < 1$, then the spectrum has the appearance shown in figure 3.6 where it can be seen that there are only two significant sidebands and thus the spectrum looks the same as for an AM carrier.

If $m = 1$, then the spectrum has the appearance shown in figure 3.7: the number of significant sidebands has increased to four. If $m = 3$, then the spectrum has the appearance shown in figure 3.8: the number of significant sidebands has increased to eight. It can be inferred that the number of significant sidebands in an FM transmission is given by $2(m + 1)$. Thus the practical bandwidth of an FM signal is given by the number of significant sidebands multiplied by the width of each sideband (i.e. f_i):

FM bandwidth = $2(m + 1) f_i = 2(\Delta f_c/f_i + 1) f_i = 2 (\Delta f_c + f_i)$

Stated in words:

> The bandwidth of an FM waveform is twice the sum of the frequency deviation and the maximum frequency in the information.

- An FM transmission is a constant-power wave, regardless of the information signal and of the modulation index m, because it is operated at a

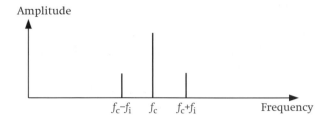

- **Figure 3.6** The spectrum of an FM wave for $m < 1$; it has the same appearance as that for an AM wave.

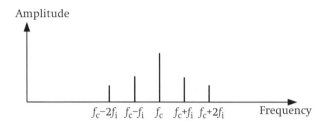

- **Figure 3.7** The spectrum of an FM wave for $m = 1$.

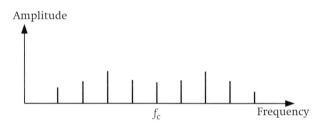

- **Figure 3.8** The spectrum of an FM wave for $m = 3$.

constant amplitude with symmetrical changes in frequency.

- As m increases, the relative amplitude of the carrier component decreases and may become much smaller than the amplitudes of the individual sidebands. This has the effect that a much greater proportion of the transmitted power is in the sidebands (rather than in the carrier), which is more efficient than AM.

Information transmitted using FM

When an FM system uses a low modulation index (i.e. $m < 1$) it is referred to as **narrowband FM** (figure 3.6). Some mobile-phone systems use this technique because it provides most of the advantages of FM while minimising the channel bandwidth.

When an FM system uses a high modulation index (i.e. when $\Delta m > 1$) it is referred to as **wideband FM** (figure 3.8). This is used in FM broadcasting.

FM radio

In national radio broadcasts using FM, the frequency deviation of the carrier, Δf_c, is chosen to be 75 kHz and the information baseband is the high-fidelity range 20 Hz to 15 kHz. Thus the modulation index m is 5 (i.e. 75 kHz ÷ 15 kHz) and such a broadcast requires an FM signal bandwidth given by

$$\text{FM radio bandwidth} = 2(\Delta f_c + f_{i\max})$$
$$= 2(75 + 15)$$
$$= 180 \text{ kHz}$$

Television sound

In terrestrial TV broadcasts, the video information is transmitted using AM, in order to make the most effective use of the available bandwidth. However, the sound information is transmitted using FM, in order to reduce mutual interference between video and sound. In this case, the maximum deviation of the carrier, Δf_c, is chosen to be 50 kHz and the information baseband is again the high-fidelity range 20 Hz to 15 kHz. Thus

$$\text{TV sound bandwidth} = 2(50 + 15)$$
$$= 130 \text{ kHz}$$

Satellite TV

Many satellite TV transmissions broadcast an analogue video signal using FM (in order to obtain an acceptable signal-to-noise ratio from very distant transmitters – see the next section). In this case the frequency deviation of the carrier Δf_c is chosen to be about 10 MHz; with a baseband video signal of about 5 MHz the bandwidth is then given by

$$\text{Satellite TV bandwidth} = 2(10 + 5)$$
$$= 30 \text{ MHz}$$

Note that an increasing number of satellite broadcasting companies are changing from analogue to digital formats (i.e. from frequency modulation to pulse code modulation – see chapter 4).

SAQ 3.2

A 10 MHz carrier is frequency modulated by a pure signal tone of frequency 8 kHz. The frequency deviation is 32 kHz. Calculate the bandwidth of the resulting FM waveform.

Comparison of AM and FM

Five points in favour of FM:

- All communication signals pick up interference and noise and these mostly affect the amplitude of the carrier. In an AM system (where the information is contained in the amplitude) the noise adds to the information and thus pollutes it. In an FM system, however, there is no information contained in the amplitude of the carrier and thus any noise picked up can be wiped off at the receiver (i.e. FM is inherently less noisy than AM). Thus the signal to noise ratio is greater for FM than for AM.
- In a wideband FM signal, the amplitude of the carrier component is relatively small: most of the transmitted power goes into the sidebands, where the information is carried. Thus FM is a much more efficient process than AM.
- In wideband FM, the dynamic range (the ratio of the largest and smallest amplitudes) of the information signal can be much greater than with AM.
- In wideband FM, the FM receiver can reject the weaker of two similar frequency signals picked up by its aerial. This is called the **capture effect**.
- Using FM, it is possible to transmit the same quality of information using a lower-power transmitter.

Two points against FM:

- The modulators and demodulators for FM are more complex than for AM.
- The FM bandwidth needed for a given information baseband is greater than that for AM.

You might wonder why AM is still used by broadcasters when FM is clearly the superior system, i.e. the points in favour of FM might appear to outweigh the points against. The dominating factor, however, is bandwidth: in telecommunications, bandwidth is a precious commodity. The important fact is that wideband FM requires a much greater bandwidth than AM to transmit the same information and this places restrictions on its use.

SUMMARY

◆ Modulation is the process of adding information onto a carrier.

◆ The baseband is the range of frequencies present in the information signal.

◆ In AM the information is contained in the variations of carrier amplitude.

◆ In FM the information is contained in the variations of carrier frequency.

◆ AM generates a carrier and two sidebands.

◆ FM generates a carrier and multiple sidebands.

◆ AM bandwidth is 2 × maximum information signal frequency.

◆ FM bandwidth is 2 × sum of frequency deviation and maximum signal frequency.

◆ The signal-to-noise ratio is much better for FM than AM.

◆ FM is a more efficient process than AM.

◆ FM can have a greater dynamic range than AM.

◆ The required bandwidth for FM is much greater than for AM.

Questions

1 *Figure 3.9* shows an AM carrier modulated by a pure tone. Calculate the carrier frequency and the pure tone frequency, and then sketch the frequency spectrum of the AM signal.

2 A radio station on the MW network transmits with a carrier frequency of 500 kHz amplitude modulated by an audio baseband of 100 Hz to 3.5 kHz. Sketch the frequency spectrum of the station and calculate the bandwidth of the AM signal.

3 Suggest why it would not be sensible for long-wave radio transmitters operating in the range 140 kHz to 280 kHz to use FM.

4 *Figure 3.10* shows an FM carrier modulated by a pure tone. Calculate the carrier frequency and the pure tone frequency.

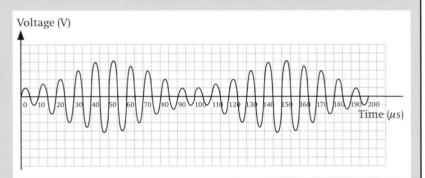

● **Figure 3.9**

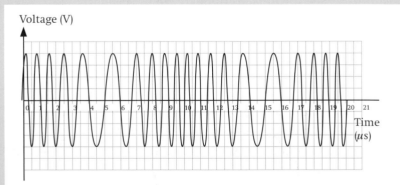

● **Figure 3.10**

5 An audio signal, with a baseband of 200 Hz to 4 kHz, frequency modulates a carrier of frequency 50 MHz. The frequency deviation per volt is 10 kHz V^{-1} and the maximum audio voltage it can transmit is 3 V. Calculate the frequency deviation and the bandwidth of the FM signal.

CHAPTER 4

Pulse code modulation

By the end of this chapter you should be able to:

1 understand that the *digital transmission* of speech or music involves analogue-to-digital conversion on transmission and digital-to-analogue conversion on reception;

2 describe how an analogue waveform may be *sampled* and encoded in binary form as a digital signal using an analogue-to-digital converter (ADC);

3 understand the effect of the sampling rate on the output signal;

4 understand how the individual samples become a stream of pulses by *parallel-to-serial* conversion;

5 understand how the analogue information signal is recovered from the pulse stream at the receiver;

6 understand the connection between bandwidth and *bit rate*;

7 understand how a carrier wave is *keyed* to carry the digital signal;

8 describe how the bit rate of a channel can be increased by quadrature amplitude modification.

Transmitting analogue signals in digital form

To transmit digitally an analogue signal such as speech or music, the analogue signal must be regularly **sampled**. The stream of samples is then converted into digital form, i.e. **digitised**, by an **analogue-to-digital converter** (ADC). This process is known as **pulse code modulation**. On reception of the digital signal, digital-to-analogue conversion takes place. It was explained in chapter 2 that an ADC is an integrated circuit (IC) that has one input pin, which accepts an analogue voltage of any value, and n output pins, which produce a corresponding n-bit binary number. *Figure 4.1* shows how this IC can be used to transmit an analogue signal in digital form.

The **sample-and-hold circuit** repeatedly samples and stores, for a brief period, the value of the analogue voltage at some moment in time (remember that the analogue signal varies

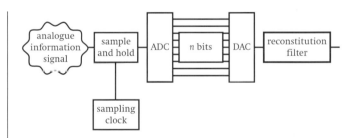

● **Figure 4.1** The conversion and recovery of an analogue signal.

continuously with time). The rate at which such samples are taken is governed by the frequency of the sampling clock.

The ADC converts each sample of the analogue information into a code of n bits. These n-bit codes are transmitted in parallel along n wires, one sample after another, to a matching n-bit digital-to-analogue converter (DAC). This produces a stepped analogue voltage from the incoming codes (*figures 2.10* and *2.12*). The output is often referred to as a **staircase approximation** to the original analogue signal.

The **reconstitution filter** is essentially a filter circuit that smoothes out the quantisation steps from the DAC. It operates in such a way that it appears to guess, or interpolate, the value of the analogue signal between samples.

The ability of this system to transmit and recover the original analogue information is dependent on the **sampling rate** (**sampling frequency**) relative to the information frequency. To illustrate this effect, *figure 4.2a* shows a sinusoidal information signal (i.e. a pure tone) of frequency 500 Hz; *figure 4.2b* shows the result of sampling every 2.5 ms (i.e. the sampling frequency is 400 Hz); *figure 4.2c* shows the reconstituted output.

It can be seen that the recovered information signal is not at all like the original. Indeed, the original signal has been lost and a lower-frequency signal has replaced it. This lower-frequency signal is called an **alias** and has appeared because the sampling frequency is far too low. Great care must be taken to avoid aliasing when converting analogue signals into digital. A well-known example of aliasing is the stroboscopic appearance of stage coach wheels in a cinema film when the sampling frequency (i.e. that of the camera, 24 frames per second) is too low to recover the information (i.e. the frequency at which spokes pass 12 o'clock is about 16 per second). In 1924, the Dutch mathematician Harry Nyquist first showed that to recover an information signal from a series of samples, the sampling frequency must be greater than twice the maximum frequency f_{max} in the information. This is known as the **sampling theorem** and the frequency $2f_{max}$ is known as the **Nyquist frequency**.

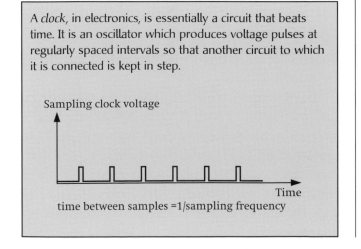

A *clock*, in electronics, is essentially a circuit that beats time. It is an oscillator which produces voltage pulses at regularly spaced intervals so that another circuit to which it is connected is kept in step.

Sampling clock voltage

Time
time between samples =1/sampling frequency

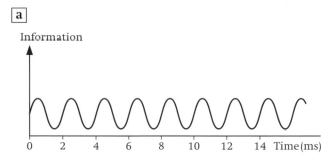

a

Information

0   2   4   6   8   10   12   14   Time (ms)

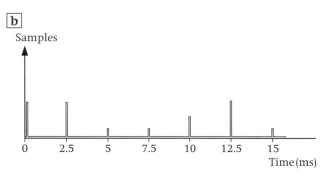

b

Samples

0   2.5   5   7.5   10   12.5   15
Time (ms)

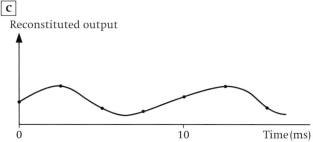

c

Reconstituted output

0   10   Time (ms)

● **Figure 4.2 a** Pure-tone information signal, period 2 ms; **b** the signal as sampled at intervals of 2.5 ms; **c** the reconstituted output.

Figure 4.3 shows the same 500 Hz information signal as in *figure 4.2* but this time sampled at a frequency of 2 kHz (i.e. greater than the Nyquist frequency, which is 2 × 500 Hz). The recovered output can clearly be seen to be a rough copy of the original.

When the analogue signal to be sampled and digitised has a range of frequencies, it is essential to pass it through a **bandpass filter** before sampling. In this way, all the frequencies that are too high for the given sampling rate are removed, so that no aliases are generated (*figure 4.4*).

Anti-alias examples

■ In the **telephone system**, as explained in chapter 2, voice frequencies are restricted to the range 300 Hz to 3.4 kHz. Thus the bandpass filter is set up to pass only this range of frequencies to the sample-and-hold circuit. The sampling

Information

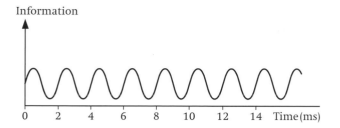

Samples

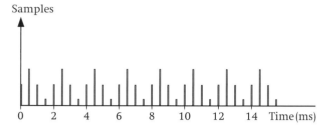

Reconstituted output

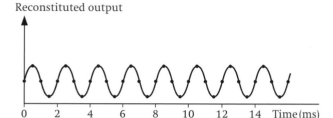

● **Figure 4.3 a** Pure-tone information signal, period 2 ms; **b** the signal as sampled at 2 kHz, i.e. at intervals of 0.5 ms; **c** the reconstituted output. The Nyquist criterion is satisfied.

frequency is 8000 Hz, which satisfies the Nyquist criterion of being greater than twice 3.4 kHz, the maximum baseband frequency.

■ When making a **compact disc**, the recording studio passes the music signal through a band-pass filter that limits the maximum frequency to 20 kHz. Sampling is then taken at a frequency of 44.1 kHz, which again satisfies the Nyquist criterion of being greater than twice the 20 kHz maximum.

SAQ 4.1_____

An audio signal has a baseband that ranges from 0.5 kHz to 4.5 kHz. If this signal is to be digitised, state which of the following frequencies would be a suitable sampling frequency:
4.0 kHz, 5.0 kHz, 6.8 kHz, 8.2 kHz, 9.8 kHz, 18 kHz

Parallel to serial

In *figure 4.4*, parallel transmission of the information takes place between the transmitter and the receiver. This means that the n bits of code are simultaneously sent down n separate wires at a rate governed by the frequency of the sampling clock. Although this is the fastest (and simplest) method by which a digital signal can be transferred, it is not viable when the transmission distance is more than a few metres. There are two reasons for this.

■ The cost of a long cable composed of n wires would be high.
■ The transmitted digital signal would suffer from **skew**: each bit of an n-bit word takes a slightly different time to travel along its individual wire. As the cable becomes longer and longer the effect worsens, and the n bits received at any moment in time may not be the same as the n bits originally transmitted.

Consequently, the parallel transmission of digital data is only used where fast data transfer is required over short distances, for example in the link between a computer and a printer.

The alternative is to use a single conductor for the data transfer. *Figure 4.5* shows the basic arrangement for transmitting the n bits of code along a single conductor. These n bits of code from the ADC are input to an electronic circuit known as a **parallel-to-serial shift register**. This circuit

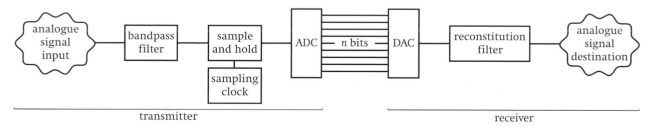

● **Figure 4.4** Analogue conversion and transmission in n-bit binary.

swallows the entire n-bit word on one clocking pulse and then transmits it, one bit at a time (under the control of another clocking pulse). These n bits progress along the single conductor to the receiver and it is in this single conductor that the **digital signal** exists. If a serially transmitted digital signal is examined on an oscilloscope then it is observed to be an apparently random procession of 1s and 0s, as shown in *figure 4.6.*

At the other end of the single conductor is a receiver containing a **serial-to-parallel shift register**. This circuit swallows the bits as they arrive, one after the other, and temporarily stores them. Once it has received all n bits, it outputs the entire n-bit word in parallel to a DAC (to recover the original analogue signal).

> The process of sampling an analogue signal, converting each sample into a word of n bits and transmitting each bit serially is called **pulse code modulation** (PCM).

Receiving a digital signal

In a PCM system, the parallel-to-serial and serial-to-parallel circuits have to work fast, because they must swallow and shift the n bits of each sample

before the next n-bit sample arrives for transmission. That is to say, the control clocks for the parallel-to-serial and serial-to-parallel circuits have to run at a much faster rate than the original sampling clock.

There are three basic problems for the serial-to-parallel receiving circuit in all digital transmission systems. These are as follows.

- How does the receiver know when a data sample (a word) begins and ends?
- How does the receiver know which bit is which within the sample?
- How does the receiver know when to swallow the next bit in a sample?

The possible solutions to these problems in recognition and timing may be broadly categorised as either asynchronous or synchronous.

Asynchronous transmission

This is normally used for the intermittent transmission of data over short distances, such as the link between a computer and a datalogger. The data sample is relatively short and extra bits are added to the sample to act as START bits and STOP bits. Sometimes, the transmitter adds a **parity** bit to the sample so that the receiver can

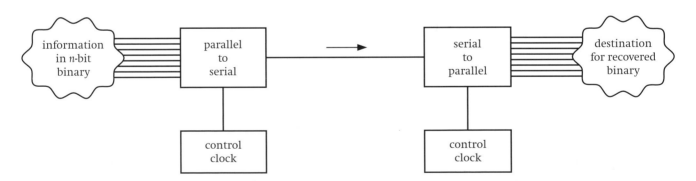

● **Figure 4.5** Serial transmission of binary information.

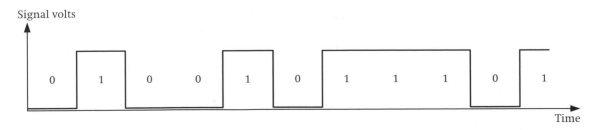

● **Figure 4.6** A typical digital signal.

perform simple error checking. If the number of 1s in the data sample is odd then the parity bit is made 1, but if the number of 1s in the data sample is even then the parity bit is made 0. In this way, the receiver can expect always to receive an even number of high, or logic 1, bits. (If it does not receive an even number, then the data sample can be retransmitted.) A typical short-distance asynchronous digital signal is shown in *figure 4.7* and an explanation of the process is given below.

1 The single transmission wire or conductor (the **line**) is held at logic 1 (high) until the system is ready to transmit.
2 The first bit placed on the line by the parallel-to-serial transmitter is a START bit of logic 0. Thus, as soon as the receiver notices the line has gone low, it knows that a series of bits is about to arrive.
3 The first bit to arrive is the least significant of the data sample.
4 The receiver clock is arranged to run at a similar speed to that of the transmitter so that at intervals of the **bit duration** τ, successive bits are swallowed.
5 The receiver is pre-programmed to expect the appropriate number of bits up to the most significant bit.
6 The final bit is the STOP bit, which forces the

line high again (some systems have two STOP bits to introduce a longer gap between transmissions).
7 The line stays high until the next word is ready to be transmitted.

Synchronous transmission

In synchronous transmission, the information is organised and sent in a regular and continuous way to the receiver. It is used for long-distance transmissions of digitised telephone calls and Internet data. Successive data samples (words) are grouped into a long stream or **block of data**. The block of data is preceded in time by a **header**, which contains information so that the receiver is able to accept the data block in the correct order (this will be explained further in chapter 11). The entire digital stream of 1s and 0s in the header and data block is called a **frame**. This is shown in *figure 4.8*.

It is essential in synchronous transmission systems that the receiving clock operates at exactly the same rate as that of the transmitter and there are several ways in which this can be achieved. For example, long-distance digital signals are often not simply coded as low for 0 and high for 1. This is because in a sample such as, say, 0011111001, the line into the receiver would be

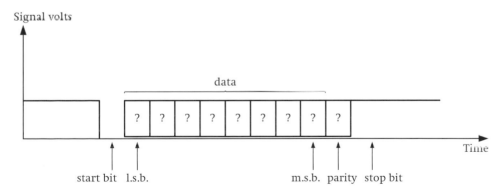

● **Figure 4.7** Asynchronous transmission; the symbol ? can equal either 1 or 0.

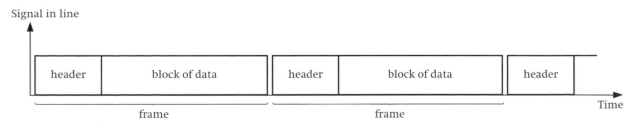

● **Figure 4.8** Synchronous transmission.

high for a relatively long time during the 11111 section and the receiving clock could easily get out of step without some other means of synchronisation. However, if the bits are coded on to the carrier according to the **Manchester Coding** system, then the carrier signal always changes state (1 to 0 or 0 to 1) in the middle of each and every bit interval. Such a coding system therefore generates its own clock to which the receiver can easily synchronise. The reader is referred to more advanced texts for a fuller explanation of synchronous transmission.

Bit rate of digital signals

A digital signal in which the bits are transmitted serially, one bit after the other, is characterised by a **bit rate**. The bit rate is simply the number of bits (either 1 or 0) that are transmitted per second; it may be calculated from

$$\text{bit rate} = \frac{1}{\tau} \qquad (\text{where } \tau = \text{bit duration})$$

Alternatively, this quantity can be calculated from

$$\text{bit rate} = \text{sampling frequency} \times \\ \text{number of bits per sample}$$

Audio CD

When making an audio CD, the recording studio samples the left and right signals 44 100 times per second: each sample is composed of a 16-bit word for the left signals and a 16-bit word for the right. The bits are stored serially on the CD so that they may be replayed at a later date. This is shown in *figure 4.9*.

The rate at which bits are added to the CD (during recording) or removed from the CD (during playback) is given by

$$\text{CD bit rate} = 44\,100 \times 2 \times 16 \\ = 1\,411\,200 \text{ bits per second}$$

Telephone

All telephone calls nowadays are sampled 8000 times per second. Each sample is an eight-bit word representing the analogue voltage of the call at the instant in time at which the sample was taken. The system is shown in *figure 4.10,* where the similarities to the CD system should be noted, i.e. a CD can be imagined to be a sophisticated answer-phone that stores audio information (on a disc) from which it is extracted when required.

$$\text{Telephone bit rate} = 8000 \times 8 \\ = 64\,000 \text{ bits per second}$$

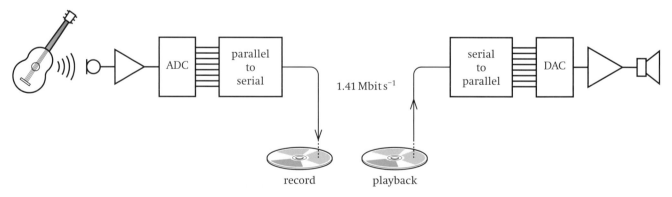

● **Figure 4.9** A compact disc (CD) audio system.

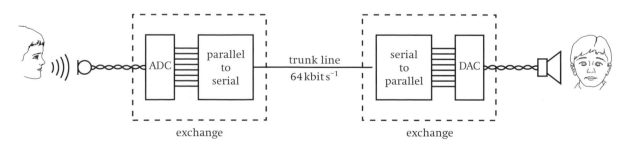

● **Figure 4.10** Digital signals in the telephone system.

SAQ 4.2

A data-logger took 200 samples per second from an experiment that lasted for 30 seconds. Each sample was 12 bits in length. Calculate the data-logger bit rate and the total number of bits stored by the data-logger.

Bandwidth of a digital signal

A digital signal, transmitted in serial form along a line, is just as likely to be at logic 1 as at logic 0. Although such a square-wave signal generates an infinite bandwidth, most of the power is contained in frequencies below the bit rate. *Figure 4.11* shows a digital signal and the corresponding power spectrum for **unipolar** pulses (i.e. where logic 1 is positive and logic 0 is zero rather than negative). Pulses in optic fibres, for example, are unipolar because the pulses have to be either positive (laser on) or zero (laser off). However, a digital transmission line, whether cable, radio or optic fibre, cannot have an infinite bandwidth, so what is the minimum bandwidth that will allow the digital signal to pass?

To answer this, consider a digital signal with a bit rate of B bits s^{-1} and a bit duration of τ. As in the case of the TV screen, chapter 2, the signal with the highest pulse frequency is a simple alternation of 1s and 0s (*figure 4.12*). As each bit lasts for τ seconds, the frequency of this pulse stream will be given by $1/(2\tau) = B/2$. Now this might suggest that the band-width of the line along which the digital signal is to progress is only required to be $B/2$ Hz, but practical limits to signalling rates usually prohibit this. Such a limited bandwidth would round off pulses to an unacceptable extent and so it is normally the case that the minimum channel bandwidth for a digital signal is the bit rate, B Hz.

Carrier modulation by digital signals

It is sometimes possible to transmit a digital signal directly, without a carrier, and this would be termed **baseband transmission**. This can happen in a short length of electrical cable, where the 1s and 0s are essentially pulses of voltage or current. Usually, however, a carrier is required to transport the bits through the wire pairs of the telephone system (in which case the carrier is a.c. current) or the atmosphere (the carrier is radio waves) or the optic fibre (the carrier is infrared light).

Note that modulation by a *digital* signal must make some property of the carrier switch between

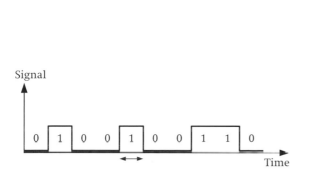
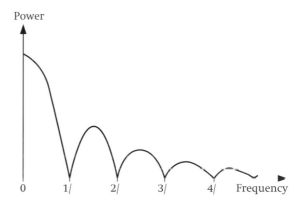

● **Figure 4.11** A unipolar-pulse digital signal and its spectrum.

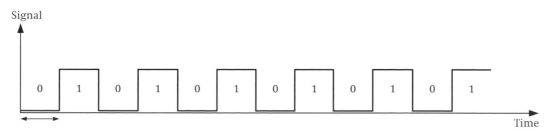

● **Figure 4.12** Bit sequence for highest-frequency pulse stream.

one state and another state (according to whether the digital information is logic 1 or logic 0); this process is known as **keying**.

Amplitude-shift keying (ASK)

In this process, the sine wave carrier is simply switched on or off, depending on whether the information is logic 1 or logic 0. As mentioned above, this method is used for the transmission of digital signals in optic fibres; it is illustrated in *figure 4.13*.

Frequency-shift keying (FSK)

In this process, two different sine-wave carrier frequencies are used alternately, to transmit the digital information. The amplitude stays constant. The higher frequency is used to represent logic 0 and the lower frequency represents logic 1. This is shown in *figure 4.14*.

Phase-shift keying (PSK)

In this process, the carrier is again a sine wave of constant amplitude. The 1s and 0s of the information are transmitted as the same frequency but in antiphase (i.e. there is a 180° phase change each time the data changes state, $0 \rightarrow 1$ or $1 \rightarrow 0$). This is shown in *figure 4.15*.

Quadrature: increasing the bit rate

The three methods described above (ASK, FSK, PSK) are arranged to communicate only two symbols (i.e. logic 0 or logic 1). The resulting digital signal bit rate will be B bit s^{-1} and, as explained above, the channel will require a bandwidth of B Hz.

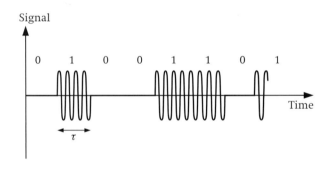
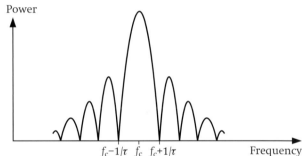

● **Figure 4.13** Amplitude-shift keying (ASK) and its spectrum.

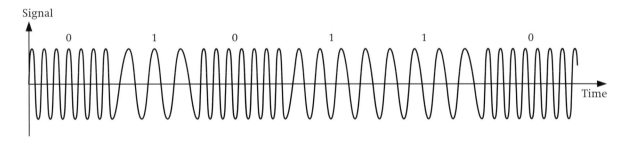

● **Figure 4.14** Frequency-shift keying (FSK).

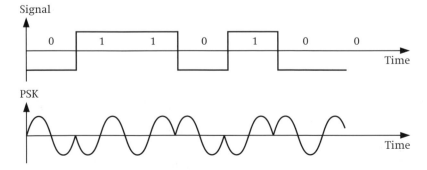

● **Figure 4.15** Phase-shift keying (PSK).

The modern telecommunications industry, however, has cleverly managed to increase the bit rate to many times B (thus increasing the rate of information transfer) without any increase in the required channel bandwidth from B Hz. It has done this by combining features of ASK and PSK, as the following example will illustrate.

Consider the following section of a digital signal that is being transferred along a channel:

0 1 1 1 0 0 0 1 1 1 1 0 0 0 1 0
1 1 1 1 0 0 0 1 1 0 1 0 0 1 0 0

Now suppose that instead of transmitting the 1s and 0s we transmit the symbols w, x, y and z. These symbols will each occupy the same time duration as one of the 1 or 0 bits above but each is made to represent two bits, according to

$$w = 00 \qquad x = 01 \qquad y = 10 \qquad z = 11$$

Thus the transmitted signal has become

x z w x z y w y z z w x y y x w

and we have transmitted the same information in half the time.

How is the carrier modulated to allow four symbols (w, x, y and z) where previously there were only two (0 and 1)? It can be done by changing the phase of the carrier by 90° instead of 180°, so that there are four possible carrier phases, 0°, 90°, 180° and 270°; the modulating process is described as **quadrature phase-shift keying** (QPSK).

The bit rate can be further increased if we invent a new group of 16 symbols, each of which represents a particular group of four bits. This could be as shown below:

a = 0000	e = 0100	i = 1000	m = 1100
b = 0001	f = 0101	j = 1001	n = 1101
c = 0010	g = 0110	k = 1010	o = 1110
d = 0011	h = 0111	l = 1011	p = 1111

Now the original digital signal of 32 bits can be transmitted as the following eight symbols:

h b o c p b k e

If each symbol occupies the same time as the original 1 or 0 we have transmitted the same information in a quarter of the time.

This form of modulation relies on changing both the amplitude and the phase of the carrier in such a way that the carrier has one of four possible amplitudes and one of four possible

phases (hence there are 4 × 4 = 16 possibilities). This is illustrated in *figure 4.16* and the procedure is known as quadrature amplitude phase-shift keying. The technique is usually referred to as **quadrature amplitude modulation** (QAM).

This process can be extended further, with ever more sophisticated modulating processes on the carrier to produce symbols that represent a larger group of bits.

Baud rate

The rate at which a carrier is modulated (i.e. the rate at which its state changes) is called its **baud rate**. Thus, in a channel carrying a digital signal, the baud rate is effectively given by

baud rate = number of symbols per second

where the symbols are explained in the section above, on quadrature. The bit rate is given by

bit rate = **bau**d rate × number of bits per symbol

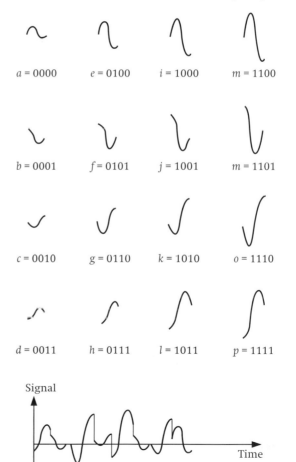

a = 0000	e = 0100	i = 1000	m = 1100
b = 0001	f = 0101	j = 1001	m = 1101
c = 0010	g = 0110	k = 1010	o = 1110
d = 0011	h = 0111	l = 1011	p = 1111

Signal

Time

h b o c p b k e

● **Figure 4.16** Quadrature amplitude modulation (QAM) signals and a signal stream.

SUMMARY

- Analogue information can be converted into digital form by regular sampling.

- The sampling frequency must be greater than twice the maximum information frequency.

- Each sample is represented by a n-bit binary code or word.

- The parallel transmission of n bits along n wires is not usually a viable system.

- Binary words are transmitted in serial form and this becomes the digital signal.

- Asynchronous transmission is used for intermittent small-word transfer over short distances.

- Synchronous transmission is used for long frames of words over long distances.

- The highest digital pulse frequency from a bit rate of B bit s^{-1} occurs when the sequence is 10101010101010 etc., giving a frequency of $B/2$ Hz.

- Keying is the process of modulating a carrier property by a digital signal.

- ASK, FSK and PSK are all digital modulation processes.

- QAM is used to increase the rate at which bits can be transmitted along a line of given bandwidth.

- The baud rate is the number of symbols transmitted per second.

- The bit rate is the product of the baud rate and the number of bits per symbol.

Questions

1 An analogue television signal has a bandwidth of 5.5 MHz. State the lowest sampling frequency that will allow this signal to be digitised.

2 A 15-minute telephone call is sampled at a rate of 8 kHz and each sample is an eight-bit word. Calculate the total number of bits produced by the call.

3 An analogue signal is sampled at a rate of 2 kHz and each sample is converted into a four-bit word. The bits are then transmitted serially along a channel. Calculate the bit rate and the maximum bit duration that will allow this system to operate.

4 A particular transmission line has a bandwidth ranging from 50 Hz to 5 kHz. Calculate the highest bit rate that can pass along the line.

5 In a FSK system, logic 0 is represented by four cycles of a 4.8 kHz carrier and logic 1 is represented by two cycles of a 2.4 kHz carrier. Calculate the corresponding bit rate.

6 In a QAM system, a symbol of four bits is transmitted every 20 µs. Calculate the baud rate and the bit rate.

CHAPTER 5

Digital versus analogue in a world of attenuation and noise

By the end of this chapter you should be able to:

1 understand and use *signal attenuation* expressed in dB per kilometre;

2 understand that *noise* is any unwanted signal superimposed on the transmitted signal;

3 appreciate the effect of noise on the quality of a signal;

4 recall and use the expression
number of decibels (dB) = $10 \lg (P_1/P_2)$
for the ratio of two power values;

5 understand and use the *gain* of an amplifier expressed in dB;

6 recall the advantages of the transmission of signals in digital form;

7 discuss the relative advantages and disadvantages of pulse code modulation.

In chapter 3 we explained how analogue information can be transmitted directly by the amplitude or frequency modulation of a continuous wave carrier. In chapter 4 we saw how the same analogue information can be converted into digital samples and then transmitted as a serial stream of pulses by modulation of a carrier (pulse code modulation). In the present chapter we concentrate on why the telecommunications industry is increasingly committed to the use of digital rather than analogue transmissions.

Attenuation

All carriers in all transmission paths suffer from attenuation; this happens regardless of the type of modulation being used or the nature of the information being carried. **Attenuation** is the progressive power loss as a signal travels along a transmission path (e.g. a wire-pair, a coaxial cable, an optic fibre or the atmosphere). The attenuation increases as the length of the transmission path increases.

In a wire-pair or coaxial cable carrying electrical signals, the attenuation is partly caused by heat losses due to currents in the cable resistance and partly by radiation transmitted from the cables, which always occurs when the charges within them undergo rapid acceleration.

In an optic fibre carrying light signals, the attenuation is partly caused by absorption of the light energy owing to impurities in the fibre.

In radio-wave broadcasts, attenuation of the electromagnetic waves is caused by losses due to induced currents in the Earth and absorption in the atmosphere and ionosphere.

The **total attenuation** (relative power loss) along a transmission path is quoted in **decibels** (see below); the **characteristic attenuation** of a transmission cable (electrical or optical) is usually quoted in decibels per kilometre.

Noise

All modern telecommunication systems involve signals (i.e. voltages and currents) in electronic circuits. In every circuit unwanted electrical energy will be present; this will add itself to the information signal. The unwanted energy may be derived from the following sources:

- **White noise** is present in all electrical circuits and is associated with the process of electrical conduction through the randomly vibrating atoms (their motion increases with temperature). White noise manifests itself as random fluctuations in voltage or current. It tends to have a constant mean power level over a wide range of frequencies.
- **Cross-talk** occurs when a transmission picks up some of the power radiated from neighbouring transmissions (it is sometimes referred to as **cross-linking**).
- **Interference** occurs when a transmission picks up atmospheric or man-made radiation, e.g. from lightning or electrical machines or unsuppressed engines.

In telecommunications, the total unwanted energy or power added to a signal is generally referred to as **noise.**

The amount of noise on a signal is usually quoted as a ratio, known as the signal-to-noise ratio. The higher the ratio, the better is the quality of the information. Like attenuation, the signal-to-noise ratio is measured in decibels (see below).

The decibel

This unit is extremely useful when comparing physical quantities that have a huge range in magnitude. Your ear, for example, can detect a sound intensity (i.e. a power per unit area) that can vary from about $10^{-12}\,\mathrm{W\,m^{-2}}$ (your threshold of hearing) to about $10\,\mathrm{W\,m^{-2}}$ (when you feel pain). So, instead of quantifying a sound intensity by its absolute magnitude (by stating, for example, that a concert generated $0.2\,\mathrm{W\,m^{-2}}$ at the back of the hall) we often compare the sound intensity with our threshold of hearing to get a measure of how much louder one sound is than the other. So, how could you compare $0.2\,\mathrm{W\,m^{-2}}$ (the concert) with

---

Logarithms

Logarithms were invented four hundred years ago by the Scottish mathematician John Napier to enable complex calculations of product (ab), quotient (a/b) and power (a^b) to be performed by the simple processes of addition, subtraction and easy multiplication respectively.

The logarithm of a number to a given base is the power to which the base must be raised to give the number.

The base chosen for the common logarithm (written as lg) is the number 10 and so we have
lg 100   = 2 (because 10^2 is the number 100)
lg 10 000= 4 (because 10^4 is the number 10 000)
lg 3981   = 3.6 (because $10^{3.6}$ is the number 3981)

The rules for using logs are as follows.

$\lg ab = \lg a + \lg b$

Thus lg $(10\,000 \times 100) = \lg 10\,000 + \lg 100$
$$= 4 + 2 = 6.$$

Compare $\lg 10^6 = 6$.

$\lg a/b = \lg a - \lg b$

Thus lg $(10\,000/100) = \lg 10\,000 - \lg 100 = 4 - 2 = 2$.
Compare $\lg 10^2 = 2$.

$\lg a^b = b \lg a$

Thus lg $1000^2 = 2 \lg 1000 = 2 \times 3 = 6$.

Compare lg $10^6 = 6$.

$10^{-12}\,\mathrm{W\,m^{-2}}$ (the quietest sound that can be heard)?

If you subtracted the two intensities, you would obtain $0.199\,999\,999\,999\,\mathrm{W\,m^{-2}}$, which is clearly too tedious to contemplate.

Worked example

What is the number A if it is given by the following equation?

$$10 \lg (A/15) = 63$$

Solution: Rearrange the equation to make A the subject:

$\lg (A/15) = 6.3$
$A/15 = 10^{6.3}$

Thus
$A = 15 \times 10^{6.3} = 29\,900\,000$

SAQ 5.1

Calculate the number P if it is given by the equation
$$10 \lg (P/42) = 16$$

If you divided the two intensities, you would obtain 2×10^{11}, which is better but is still an extremely large number to contemplate.

The **decibel** (dB) makes working with such large comparisons easy. The decibel comparison of two quantities P_1 and P_2 is defined as 10 times the logarithm of their ratio:

number of decibels (dB) = $10 \lg (P_1/P_2)$

We can now compare the sound intensity P_1 produced by the concert with the threshold of hearing P_2:

$$\text{number of dB} = 10 \lg (0.2/10^{-12}) = 10 \lg (2 \times 10^{11})$$
$$= 10 \times (\lg 2 + 11) = 10 \times (0.3 + 11)$$
$$= 113 \text{ dB}$$

and we have arrived at a number that is easy to comprehend.

SAQ 5.2

As you listen to a particular person speak, the sound intensity at your ear is $5 \times 10^{-7}\,\mathrm{W\,m^{-2}}$. Calculate the decibel comparison with the threshold intensity of hearing.

Although the decibel was originally devised for sound comparisons, it is now used extensively in telecommunications to compare two power values (where power = energy/time). The important point to remember is that the decibel is not an absolute unit. It is 10 times the logarithm of the power *ratio*. Thus it is meaningless to make a statement such as 'the signal power is 70 dB', unless it is understood that it is 70 dB above or below a particular reference power level. (In telecommunications, this reference level is commonly taken to be 1 mW.) For example, when the power of a sound is 10^4 greater than threshold, this is 40 dB.

The decibel in telecommunications

There are three important areas of application for the decibel in telecommunications. The decibel makes calculations of signal power and noise power less tedious than they would otherwise be.

- **Attenuation**

  Figure 5.1 shows a cable (it could be electrical or optic-fibre) of length L, into which is applied a signal power P_{in} and out of which emerges a smaller signal power P_{out}. The **total attenuation** of a signal in this cable can be expressed in decibels as follows:

  total attenuation of signal = $10 \lg (P_{out}/P_{in})$

  Note that this will be negative. The characteristic signal attenuation of the cable is usually expressed in decibels per kilometre as follows:

  signal attenuation per kilometre = $10 \lg (P_{out}/P_{in})/L$

  Again, the value will be negative.

- **Signal-to-noise ratio**

  Figure 5.2 shows a signal of power P_{sig} on which there is superimposed noise of power P_{noise}. The **signal-to-noise ratio** is normally expressed in decibels as follows:

  signal-to-noise ratio = $10 \lg (P_{sig}/P_{noise})$.

  This should be positive!

- **Amplifier power gain**

  Figure 5.3 shows an amplifier which accepts a small input signal of power P_{in} and which outputs a larger signal of power P_{out}. The **power gain** of this amplifier is normally expressed in decibels as follows:

  power gain = $10 \lg (P_{out}/P_{in})$

  Again, the value is expected to be positive. To apply these definitions, consider the transmission path of a typical signal, as shown in *figure 5.4*. Here, a signal of power P_{in} is applied to a cable of

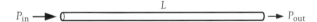

- **Figure 5.1** Attenuation in a cable of length L.

- **Figure 5.2** Signal plus noise.

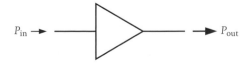

- **Figure 5.3** An amplifier.

length L and attenuation $-A$ dB km^{-1}. After travelling a distance L, the signal emerging from the cable is amplified by an amplifier of power gain G dB. Then it is transmitted a further distance L before being amplified again by a similar amplifier. This is repeated over a transmission distance of $4L$ as shown. We now ask some questions.

1 What is the total attenuation of the signal caused by the transmission cable?
  The answer is $-A \times 4L$ dB; note that it is negative.
2 What would be the power gain of the signal if it passed through the four amplifiers without any attenuation along the line?
  The answer is $4G$ dB; it will be positive.
3 What is the nett change in signal power after this transmission, taking attenuation into account?
  It can be shown that, in terms of decibel level, the competing effects of amplifier gain and attenuation are simply subtracted, so that the nett change in signal power level is equal to the gain decibels minus the attenuation decibels, $(4G - 4AL)$ dB. Note that if the gain just compensates for the loss (i.e. $4G = 4AL$), then the total change in signal power will be 0 dB. This does not mean a zero signal but that the final power out is the same as the original power in (remember that $\lg P/P = \lg 1 = 0$).
4 Why is the transmission cable in *figure 5.4* broken up into four sections, each ending with an amplifier? Why can we not transmit the signal uninterrupted for the whole distance $4L$ and then have an amplifier of gain $4G$ at the end of it (such a system is shown in *figure 5.5*)?
  The reason is as follows. As the signal travels along the cable it suffers attenuation

(see above). Furthermore, in the transmission path there is a noise power that remains more or less constant. Consequently, if the signal is left to travel without interruption, it would eventually become swamped by and lost in the noise. Except for unusual and sophisticated modulation systems, it would then not be possible to recover the signal from the noise. Breaking up the transmission system into sections allows the amplifiers to lift the signal well above the noise level.

In all transmission systems, it is essential to avoid letting the signal-to-noise ratio become too small otherwise the signal will become lost in the noise.

The amplifiers with which long-distance cables are broken up are called **repeaters**. The 13 000 km under-sea coaxial cable that links Sydney in Australia and Vancouver in Canada is broken up with 1000 repeaters, i.e. there is an amplifier every 13 kilometres.

Worked example

A signal of 450 mW is input to a cable of attenuation 6 dB km^{-1}. Calculate the power P_{out} of the signal that emerges after travelling through 4 km of this cable.

Solution: The total attenuation of the signal
$$= 6 \times (-4) = -24 \text{ dB}$$
Thus
$$-24 = 10 \lg (P_{out}/450 \times 10^{-3})$$
$$-2.4 = \lg (P_{out}/450 \times 10^{-3})$$
It follows that
$$10^{-2.4} = P_{out}/450 \times 10^{-3}$$
$$P_{out} = 10^{-2.4} \times 450 \times 10^{-3}$$
$$= 1.8 \text{ mW}$$

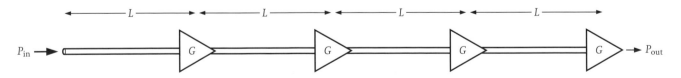

● **Figure 5.4** A long-distance transmission system.

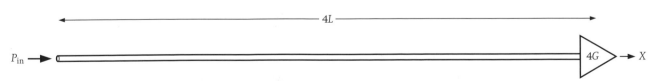

● **Figure 5.5** A non-viable transmission system.

Worked example

The signal entering an amplifier has a power of 7.6 μW and the signal leaving it is 2.4 W. Calculate the power gain in decibels of the amplifier.

Solution: The power gain $= 10 \lg (2.4/7.6 \times 10^{-6})$
$$= 55 \, \text{dB}$$

Worked example

The signal emerging from a coaxial cable has a power of 33 mW. If the signal-to-noise ratio is 22 dB calculate the noise power P_{noise} in the cable.

Solution: The signal-to-noise ratio
$$-\, 22$$
$$= 10 \lg (33 \times 10^{-3}/P_{noise})$$
Thus
$$2.2 = \lg (33 \times 10^{-3}/P_{noise})$$
$$P_{noise} = 33 \times 10^{-3}/10^{2.2}$$
$$= 0.21 \, \text{mW}$$

SAQ 5.3

A 200 mW signal enters a cable system of length 100 km. The cable has an attenuation of 8 dB km^{-1}. Amplifiers of gain 41 dB are located at 5 km intervals. Calculate:

a the total power loss of the signal as a result of travelling through the 100 km cable;

b the total signal gain as a result of passing through the 20 amplifiers in the system;

c the signal power emerging from the twentieth amplifier, at the end of the system.

Amplification and noise

If the signal in a cable is analogue (such as an AM carrier with TV information or telephone information), then the signals before and after amplification will resemble those shown in *figure 5.6*. It can be seen that the noise has been amplified as well as the signal and this effect worsens with repeated amplifications. Some filtering can be used to minimise the cumulative effects of noise, but even so, this is a fundamental problem with long-distance analogue transmissions: they are inherently noisy.

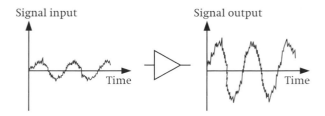

● **Figure 5.6** Amplification of an analogue signal with noise.

If, however, the signal in the cable is digital (such as modern digitised telephone information) then the signals before and after amplification can be made to resemble that shown in *figure 5.7*. The reason is that digital pulses always have a standard rectangular shape. Here it can be seen that the noise has been completely removed from the input signal which has thus been **regenerated**. The amplifier circuit that enables this to happen is called a **Schmitt trigger**. This is a two-state switching circuit that has the interesting property that the voltage required to make it switch into a high state is not the same as the voltage required to make it switch into a low state.

Figure 5.7 thus illustrates one of the most important reasons for transmitting information in digital form: no matter how far it is transmitted, or how many amplifying stages it goes through:

> A digital signal can be preserved perfectly without any distortion from the influences of channel or noise.

The advantages of digital communication

Although the principles of pulse code modulation (PCM) (i.e. sampling and digitising) were developed in 1937 by Alex Reeves, it was not until the 1970s

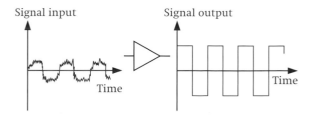

● **Figure 5.7** Amplification and regeneration of a digital signal with noise.

that the telecommunications industry began the move to digital. There were three reasons for this delay.

- Digital circuitry was much more complex than analogue circuitry.
- Early digital circuitry was expensive and unreliable (and difficult to synchronise).
- Transmission of a signal in digital form consumes a greater bandwidth than would be required to transmit in the original analogue.

The change was mainly initiated by the development of digital integrated circuits and, in particular, the microprocessor by Intel in 1971. When the electronics industry began to mass-produce low-cost, but sophisticated, chips for use in digital signal transfer, the switch to digital became inevitable.

The advantages of digital signal transfer are as follows.

- Digital signals can be perfectly regenerated.
- In long-distance transmission, noise does not accumulate on the signal with repeated amplifications.
- Digital circuits are well suited to mass production, so they have become relatively inexpensive.

- Extra codes can be added to a digital signal to check for errors in transmission.
- The bits in a digital signal can be scrambled to disguise the information. This process is called **encryption** and ensures privacy to those who have the necessary codes to unscramble the received signal.
- A greater dynamic range (maximum to minimum) of the information voltage is possible.
- Digital signals can be easily **companded**. This is the process of reducing the dynamic range at the transmitter (by **com**pression) and increasing it at the receiver (by ex**pan**sion).
- Digital signals are easily controlled, filtered, checked, encrypted, etc. by fast, modern computers.
- Digital signals are easily stored by computers in memories (both temporary RAM and permanent ROM).
- Digital signals from a huge number of different sources can be made to share the same transmission path by time-division multiplexing (see chapter 6).
- Digital signals can be compressed to eliminate redundancies in information.

SUMMARY

- All signals in all transmission paths suffer from attenuation.

- Attenuation causes the power in the signal to become less and less.

- Noise is any unwanted energy in a signal and is present in all electronic systems.

- The long-distance transmission of a signal involves repeated amplifications, to avoid losing the signal in the noise.

- All transmission systems have a minimum signal-to-noise ratio.

- The decibel is an important unit for comparing two power values. It is used for attenuation, signal-to-noise ratio and amplifier gain.

- Long-distance analogue AM transmissions are inherently noisy.

- Digital signal transfer is a superior process to analogue signal transfer.

- Noise can be removed from digital signals.

- Digital circuits are no longer expensive, lend themselves to computer control and allow a very large number of different signals in a transmission channel.

Questions

1 A signal of 25 µW enters an amplifier with a gain of 36 dB. Calculate the output power of the amplifier.

2 At the output of an amplifier there is a signal-to-noise ratio of 60 dB. How many times is the signal power greater than the noise power?

3 A signal of power 2.8 W is applied to a cable of attenuation 6.8 dB km^{-1}. The constant noise power in the cable is 8.0 µW and the signal-to-noise ratio must not fall below 35 dB. Calculate the maximum length of uninterrupted cable that may be used to transmit the signal.

4 A signal of power 64 mW enters a cable of length 15 km. At the end of the cable is an amplifier with a power gain of 60 dB. If the cable has an attenuation of 4.2 dB km^{-1} calculate the signal power that emerges from the amplifier.

CHAPTER 6

Multiplexing and the use of the radio-wave spectrum

By the end of this chapter you should be able to:

1 understand the need for *multiplexing* in telecommunication systems;

2 understand the principles of *time-division multiplexing*;

3 understand the principles of *frequency-division multiplexing*;

4 appreciate the extent and use of the radio-wave spectrum;

5 recall the wavelengths used in different modes of radio communication;

6 understand the principle of use of the *half-wave dipole aerial* as a transmitting and receiving antenna;

7 understand the use of *parabolic reflecting dishes* in transmission and reception.

Multiplexing

Suppose we want to set up a radio station to broadcast audio information to a surrounding area. The simplest possible system would convert the audio into an electrical signal using a microphone and then amplify this signal using an audio frequency (AF) amplifier. The amplifier output would then be connected to an aerial that would convert the electrical signal into electromagnetic waves of the same frequencies as the original sound waves. This arrangement is shown in *figure 6.1*.

There are three fundamental difficulties with this simple radio system.

■ Only one radio station can operate in the area, because any others would interfere with the first (unless they all agreed to transmit at different times of the day, in which case they would effectively have set up a simple form of time-division multiplexing).

■ The aerial required to transmit frequencies in the audio range (i.e. 20 Hz to 20 kHz) would have to be extremely large (many kilometres in length).

■ The amplifier would have to be enormously powerful because electromagnetic waves at low audio frequencies do not travel very far unless they have huge amplitudes (although such waves are used for communicating with submarines).

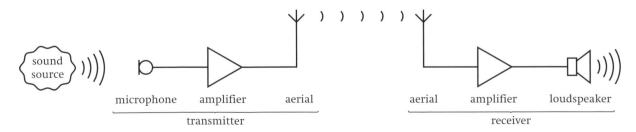

microphone   amplifier   aerial   aerial   amplifier   loudspeaker

transmitter   receiver

● **Figure 6.1** A simple radio broadcast system.

All three of these problems can be solved by the use of multiplexing. This is the process of allowing several independent users to share the same transmission medium (or link). The medium can be a cable (i.e. wire-pair, coaxial, optic-fibre) or the atmosphere (or space). An information 'pathway' within this medium is called a **channel**. By means of multiplexing, many channels can be accommodated within one single medium.

There are two basic forms of multiplexing, and these are known as time-division multiplexing (TDM) and frequency-division multiplexing (FDM). In order to understand these two processes it is essential to recall the meaning of bandwidth, as explained in chapter 2. The important idea is that any voltage signal can be represented as a function of time (i.e. as an oscilloscope trace) or as a function of frequency (i.e. in a spectrum).

Time-division multiplexing

In time-division multiplexing (TDM), each user is allocated the entire frequency band of the channel but only for a limited time slot. When this time is up, another user gains access, also for a limited time, and then another and another. Eventually, the process repeats and the original user is allowed another time slot, again followed in succession by those of the other users. This is shown for four users in *figure 6.2*.

Time-division multiplexing is perfectly suited to digital signals, where the information is already broken up into samples or blocks of data. It is arranged that each sample can be fitted into the available time slot, and the rate at which access to the channel is repeated is arranged to be the sampling rate.

For example, suppose that the real time required to speak a sentence over the telephone system is 10 seconds. When the sentence is digitised by pulse code modulation (PCM), the total number of bits produced will be 640 000 (i.e. 10 seconds × 8000 samples per second × 8 bits per sample; see chapter 4). If each bit lasts for 0.01 μs then the digitised information could be transmitted in 6.4 ms. That is, the 10 second sentence only requires the channel for 6.4 ms. Hence time in the transmission channel is wasted unless several other signals are sent down it.

Time-division multiplexing is used for digital signals because digital samples can be fitted into allocated time slots. It will be explained further in chapter 9.

Frequency-division multiplexing

In frequency-division multiplexing (FDM), each user is allocated a limited frequency band within the channel but for the entire time they wish to use it. This is shown for four users in *figure 6.3*.

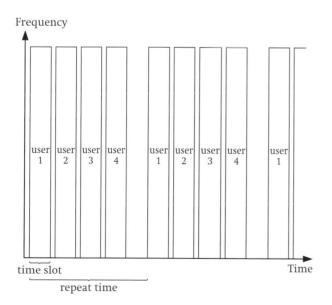

● **Figure 6.2** Time-division multiplexing (TDM).

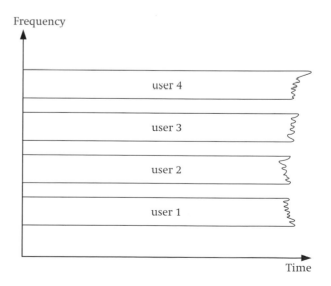

● **Figure 6.3** Frequency-division multiplexing (FDM).

FDM involves shifting the information signal (i.e. the baseband) to a higher frequency by the techniques of amplitude modulation (AM) or frequency modulation (FM), as explained in chapter 3. Thus the radio broadcast system for four radio stations, all broadcasting independently in the same area, now becomes that shown in *figure 6.4*.

Each radio station is allocated a different carrier frequency and each carrier is then

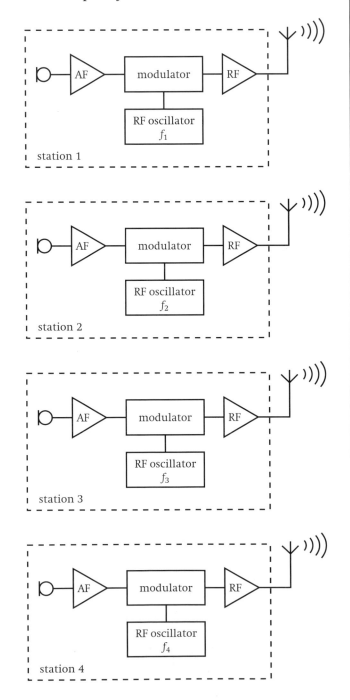

• **Figure 6.4** Four radio stations broadcasting independently in the same area.

modulated by the station's particular information. The resulting AM or FM signal is amplified by a radio frequency (RF) amplifier before being passed to the transmission aerial for broadcast. Thus the only essential difference between one radio station and another is their carrier frequencies.

The frequency spectrum of the channel (i.e. the region surrounding the four transmitters) will be of the form shown in *figure 6.5*, where it has been assumed that the four stations are using AM.

As long as there is a gap in the frequency spectrum between the transmissions of each radio station then they will not interfere with each other (i.e. adjacent carriers must be separated in frequency by more than the bandwidth of each transmission).

The above discussion shows how FDM applies to four radio stations, but the same principles apply to the entire world of telecommunications. These radio stations could be any other transmitters of information that use electromagnetic waves as the carrier. Each transmitter is allocated a specific carrier frequency and the information being carried (whether audio, video or data) is contained in the sidebands surrounding the carrier in frequency space.

Frequency-division multiplexing is used for **analogue** signals because the baseband information can be shifted by AM or FM into the allocated frequency slot.

Radio waves

When electromagnetic waves are generated (and controlled) by electronic oscillator circuits (see the section below on aerials), then these e.m. waves are referred to as **radio waves**. The frequencies at which radio waves can be generated have been steadily increasing, from a few kilohertz one hundred years ago to a few terahertz (10^{12} Hz) now. Indeed, radio waves at terahertz frequencies (called T waves) are at the forefront of present technology; the present type of source (the resonant tunnel diode) can generate a few μW of power. Note that even state-of-the-art transistor circuits cannot generate frequencies much above 300 GHz.

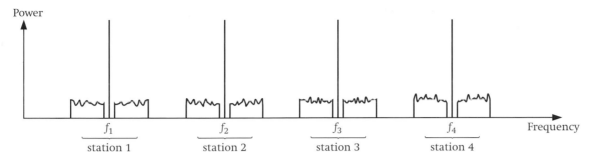

● **Figure 6.5** The combined power spectrum in the area around the four radio stations in *figure 6.4*.

Note also that although visible light is an electromagnetic wave it would not fall into the category of radio waves, because it cannot (yet) be generated by electronic oscillator circuits; these would need to operate at 10^{14} Hz!

Radio-wave spectrum

By international agreement, the radio-wave spectrum has been divided into frequency bands, each new band being an order of magnitude greater than the one before it. A list of these bands and the communication systems that use them is shown in *table 6.1* overleaf. In the UK, the government body responsible for the allocation of civil licenses as well as the maintenance and supervision of the radio-wave spectrum is called the Radiocommunications Agency (RA). The RA can be accessed on the Internet at http://www.radio.gov.uk.

The number of transmitters that can share the same radio waveband by the process of frequency-division multiplexing is very dependent on the bandwidth required. Throughout its history, a major driving force in telecommunications has been the need to maximise the number of users who share any waveband: we have

maximum number of users in waveband

$$= \frac{\text{bandwidth of waveband}}{\text{bandwidth of each user}}$$

Thus, an FM radio station, which requires a bandwidth of 180 kHz (see chapter 3), would not be allowed to broadcast in the low frequency waveband (30 kHz to 300 kHz) because then one station would have commandeered the whole waveband and no other station could use it.

Similarly, if terrestrial TV stations transmitted video information using FM rather than AM then each station would require a bandwidth of about 30 MHz (see chapter 3) and carriers would need to be separated by about 32 MHz. This is four times greater than the 8 MHz separation presently used for AM, so there would be four times fewer TV frequencies to allocate. However, if the FM TV signal is broadcast in the SHF region of the spectrum (3 GHz to 30 GHz), then the 32 MHz separation is not such a problem because there is so much more bandwidth available for the same dynamic range of the information voltage.

Worked example

AM radio stations produce sidebands of about ±4 kHz on either side of their carrier, and so it is necessary to space carriers 9 kHz apart. Calculate the maximum number of such stations that could share the LF waveband.

Solution: From *table 6.1*, the LF waveband is 30–300 kHz. Thus

maximum number = (300 kHz − 30 kHz)/9 kHz

$$= 270/9$$
$$= 30$$

If such stations were allowed to operate in the VHF waveband, calculate the maximum number that could share it.

Solution: Again using *table 6.1*,

maximum number = (300 MHz − 30 MHz)/9 kHz

$$= 270 \times 10^6/9 \times 10^3$$
$$= 30\,000$$

This shows the much greater width of the VHF band.

Frequency band	Classification	Abbreviation	Wavelength	Typical uses
3 Hz–30 Hz	extremely low	ELF	10^5–10^4 km	submarine communication
30 Hz–300 Hz	ultra-low	ULF	10^4–10^3 km	submarine communication
300 Hz–3 kHz	infra-low	ILF	10^3–10^2 km	baseband telephone signals
3 kHz–30 kHz	very low	VLF	10^2–10 km	long-range navigation
30 kHz–300 kHz	low	LF	10–1 km	long-range navigation AM radio broadcasting
300 kHz–3 MHz	medium	MF	1–0.1 km	maritime radio direction finding AM radio broadcasting

3 MHz–30 MHz	high	HF	100–10 m	international
				  radio broadcasting
				amateur radio
				long-distance
				  ship communication

30 MHz–300 MHz	very high	VHF	10–1 m	FM radio broadcasting television broadcasting aircraft communication aircraft navigational aids
300 MHz–3 GHz	ultra-high	UHF	1–0.1 m	television broadcasting mobile phones microwave links navigational aids radar
3 GHz–30 GHz	super-high	SHF	10–1 cm	mobile phones radar microwave links satellite communications
30 GHz–300 GHz	extremely high	EHF	1–0.1 cm	radar radio astronomy
300 GHz–3 THz	tremendously high	THF	1–0.1 mm	research

● **Table 6.1** The radio-wave spectrum.

SAQ 6.1

The government of an isolated island in the Pacific decides to allocate the radio spectrum from 360 MHz to 480 MHz for terrestrial TV transmissions. Each TV channel is contained within an 8 MHz bandwidth. Calculate the maximum number of TV stations that could transmit on this island.

Aerials

Radio waves are produced and detected by aerials (or antennae). An aerial can be produced in a variety of shapes and sizes depending on the following considerations.

■ Is the aerial to be used for transmitting or receiving (some will do both jobs equally well)?
■ Is it to be used for broadcasting to, or receiving from, all directions or one particular direction?
■ At which frequency or frequencies will it operate?

A transmitting aerial (or antenna) is required to launch modulated e.m. waves into the atmosphere and a receiving aerial is required to pick them up. Each aerial is a **transducer** that converts alternating currents into e.m. waves or e.m. waves into alternating currents. Thus all aerials have to be made from conductors.

When a current flows in a conductor, a magnetic field encircles the conductor (*figure 6.6*). If the direction of current changes, then the direction of magnetic field changes. A changing

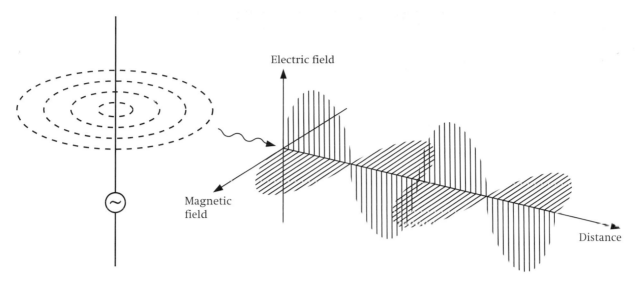

Electric field

Magnetic field

Distance

● **Figure 6.6** In the left-hand part of the diagram, the broken circles show the varying magnetic field resulting from the oscillating current in the aerial. The changes in these flux lines give rise to vertical loops of induced electric field around the flux lines.

Electromagnetic waves at radio frequencies f propagate away from an aerial and travel through space at the speed of light ($c = 3 \times 10^8\,\mathrm{m\,s^{-1}}$). Like all waves, they are governed by the equation

$$c = f\lambda$$

where f is the frequency of the a.c. current in the aerial (i.e. the carrier frequency) and λ is the wavelength of the resulting wave.

magnetic field induces an electric field, and this electric field only exists while the magnetic field is changing. With each reversal of current, some of the energy in the electric and magnetic fields is radiated away from the conductor in the form of an **electromagnetic wave**. *Figure 6.6* shows an a.c. current in a simple aerial and the corresponding e.m. wave, frozen at some moment in time.

The efficiency of an aerial, i.e. its ability to convert a.c. current into e.m. waves, is very dependent on the size and shape of the conductor. All transmission aerials have to be longer than $\lambda/10$, otherwise they are very inefficient. This is a problem not in the higher-frequency wavebands, where λ is relatively small, but in the lower-frequency wavebands. If the length of the aerial is an integral number of half-wavelengths then a resonant, and therefore effective, condition is established. The most basic aerial is a half-wave dipole.

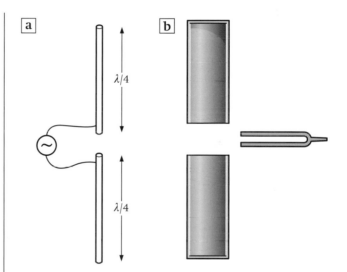

a

b

$\lambda/4$

$\lambda/4$

● **Figure 6.7 a** Half-wave dipole transmitter, driven by an a.c. generator; **b** two organ pipes, each closed at one end and open at the other, driven by a tuning fork.

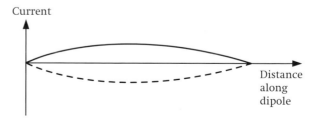

Current

Distance along dipole

● **Figure 6.8** The current in the dipole of *figure 6.7* varies between the limits shown by the solid and broken lines.

The half-wave dipole aerial

The dipole is composed of two straight conductors, each of length equal to one quarter-wavelength, separated by a short distance (*figure 6.7a*). It can be used as a transmitting or receiving aerial.

The half-wave dipole aerial is most efficient when it is being driven by or is receiving a frequency f, where $f = c/\lambda$ and λ is twice the length of the dipole. Under this resonant condition, a standing wave of current in the aerial is produced (*figure 6.8*) over the total length $\lambda/2$ of the dipole. The current at the ends is always zero and at the centre of the dipole has its most extreme positive and negative values.

It may not be obvious why there should be a current in the dipole at all, when the high-frequency generator is connected to two conductors that form an open circuit. However, remember that an alternating current in a metal is simply an oscillation of the free electrons, the strength of the current being related to the amplitude of oscillation. (It is not the case that the electrons flow all the way around a circuit in one half cycle and then all the way back again during the other.) The free electrons at the ends of the aerial are constrained not to oscillate, while those near the centre of the aerial have a maximum amplitude of oscillation. This is very

similar to the behaviour of air molecules in a standing wave in two organ pipes, each closed at one end (*figure 6.7b*).

The radiation pattern (i.e. the distribution of radiated power as a function of direction) for a vertical half-wave dipole is shown in *figure 6.9*. It can be seen that the half-wave dipole transmits equally in all horizontal directions. (It also receives equally from all horizontal directions.) However, it transmits and receives much less strongly in directions away from the horizontal.

Note that when a dipole is to handle signals of as wide a bandwidth as possible (i.e. it is to be used to transmit or pick up frequencies above and below its resonant frequency), then the two conductors should be thick, i.e. rods or tubes rather than wires.

SAQ 6.2 _____

Calculate the length of the half-wave dipole required to transmit a 150 MHz carrier.

The monopole aerial

The monopole is half a dipole, mounted on an earthed plane. A transmitting aerial for AM medium-frequency radio broadcasts is in the form of a $\lambda/4$ vertical tower perhaps 75 m in height (for a carrier of 1 MHz). Such an aerial can also be used for reception; a car aerial is a common example, and is often referred to as a *whip aerial* because of its motion in the wind.

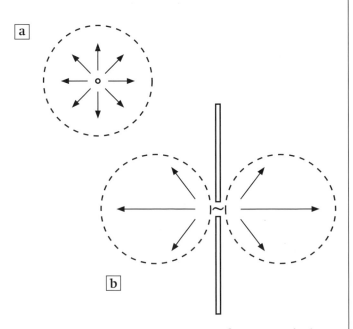

● **Figure 6.9** The radiation pattern from a vertical dipole: **a** view from above; **b** vertical elevation.

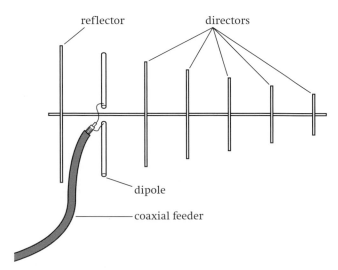

● **Figure 6.10** The Yagi-array aerial.

The Yagi-array aerial

Hidetsu Yagi was a Japanese engineer, who first demonstrated how to convert an omnidirectional dipole into one that can transmit or receive stronger signals in a particular direction. This involves adding a reflecting conductor (a reflector) that is slightly longer than half a wavelength and a number of directional conductors (directors) that are slightly shorter than half a wavelength. This is a very common type of aerial and is used for UHF television reception. A diagram of a Yagi array is shown in *figure 6.10*. (VHF radio reception is often picked up with a Yagi that has one reflector and only one director.)

Ferrite rod aerial

This is a **loop** aerial, formed by a wire coil wound around a ferrite rod. It is very useful for long wavelengths, for which a dipole would be impossibly large. The magnetic component of

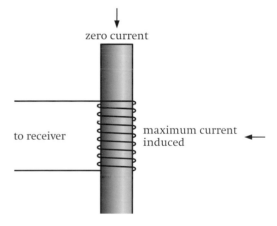

● **Figure 6.11** A ferrite-rod aerial.

incoming e.m. waves will become concentrated in the ferrite and this means a stronger changing flux, with a consequently stronger induced e.m.f. in the coil (i.e. a stronger signal received). This aerial is normally used with radio receivers that can tune in to the long-wave and medium-wave bands. A diagram of a ferrite rod aerial is shown in *figure 6.11*.

Parabolic-dish aerial

At higher frequencies, this type of aerial can be used for both transmission and reception (*figure 6.12a*). In transmission, it will produce a highly directional beam and in reception it will provide high gain from one particular direction. It consists of a metal dish in the shape of a parabola (*figure 6.12b*), with a small transmitting or receiving aerial at its focus (the **focus** of a parabola is the point to which all incident parallel radiation will converge after reflection). The transmitting and receiving aerial is often a small dipole or monopole positioned inside a **waveguide**, which is a metal tube with a circular or rectangular cross-section. An SHF signal applied to the tiny aerial results in an e.m. wave travelling along the confined space inside the tube with very little energy loss. Waveguides can be bent, to channel a signal round corners, but the bend in the tube must be carefully made. Normally, waveguides are only used for short links, such as are needed when launching a microwave from a generator into a parabolic dish for transmission.

The reason for the use of waveguides at these microwave frequencies (i.e. GHz) is that at such

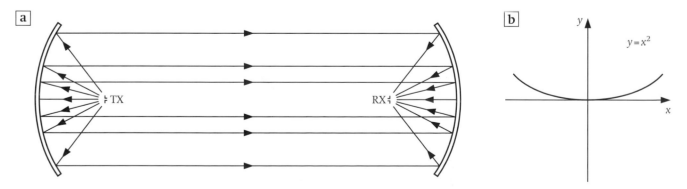

● **Figure 6.12 a** Parabolic reflector with transmitter (TX) and receiver (RX); **b** graphical representation of a parabola.

frequencies, electric current can flow only in a thin outer skin of a conductor, which therefore provides a very high resistance. Even in a coaxial cable, microwave frequencies will be highly attenuated.

Parabolic transmission

When used as a transmitter, the angular spread of the transmitted beam (called the **beamwidth**) is given in degrees by

$$\text{beamwidth} = 70\lambda/D$$

Thus, if the dish diameter D is made very much larger than the wavelength λ the beamwidth will be very small, i.e. the radiated beam will be more or less parallel.

Parabolic reception

When used as a receiver, the gain of the receiving dish is given by the equation

$$\text{gain} = 6(D/\lambda)^2$$

Note that in this case the gain does not mean the ratio of power out to power in, but the ratio of the power delivered to the dipole receiver with the dish in place to the power that the dipole would receive without the dish.

If the dish diameter D is made very much larger than the wavelength λ then the aerial will provide a very large gain. This is a very important property of the parabolic dish, because it considerably increases the signal-to-noise ratio at the receiver (i.e. the received signal at the focus is much stronger than it would be without the dish).

It is not normal to use a parabolic dish aerial with frequencies lower than about 100 MHz (when the wavelength is of the order of metres). Then the size of the required dish, which to be useful must be several times larger than λ, would make it both very expensive and potentially very unstable in high winds. Such very large dishes, however, are needed to detect very long wavelength signals in radio astronomy.

SUMMARY

- In multiplexing several users share the same transmission channel.

- Time-division multiplexing allows access to a channel in regular time slots and is used with digital signals.

- Frequency-division multiplexing allows each user a limited frequency range and is used with analogue signals.

- Radio waves are electromagnetic waves generated by electronic oscillators.

- The radio-wave spectrum ranges continuously from the lowest frequencies to terahertz.

- The radio-wave spectrum is composed of 12 frequency bands (*table 6.1*).

- The use of each of these frequency bands is governed by international agreements.

- It is normally arranged that each frequency band should have a large number of users.

- Radio waves are produced and detected by aerials.

- The half-wave dipole is a basic omnidirectional transmitting and receiving aerial.

- The Yagi array is essentially a directional dipole aerial.

- There are many different types of aerial; these are needed when a dipole is not suitable.

- The parabolic reflector is a highly directional aerial with a high gain; it is used for higher frequencies.

Questions

1 Suggest why multiplexing is essential in a telephone network.

2 Explain why FM is not used in the lower-frequency end of the radio-wave spectrum.

3 Calculate the maximum number of radio amateurs, each broadcasting a single-sideband suppressed-carrier signal of bandwidth 4 kHz, that could share the high-frequency waveband.

4 Calculate the size of dipole necessary to receive TV signals from a 375 MHz transmitter.

5 Explain, with the aid of a calculation, why it would not be practical to use a half-wave dipole as an aerial with a portable radio receiver tuned to a medium-frequency radio station.

6 Explain why modern mobile telephones have very small aerials.

7 State two ways in which parabolic dish aerials are limited.

CHAPTER 7

The propagation of radio waves and radio receivers

By the end of this chapter you should be able to:

1 describe the effect of the Earth's surface on the propagation of radio waves over long distances;

2 describe the use of the ionosphere as a *reflector* for the propagation of waves over long distances;

3 use a systems approach to explain the function of each of the following elements in a simple *amplitude-modulated radio receiver*: aerial, tuning circuit, RF amplifier, detector (demodulator), AF amplifier, loudspeaker;

4 draw a block diagram to show how the elements in a simple AM receiver are combined.

The radio waves generated by a transmitting aerial have to propagate through the atmosphere (and sometimes empty space) in order to reach a receiving aerial. Depending on their frequency, there are three modes by which such waves may reach their destination: as **surface waves**, **sky waves** or **space waves**.

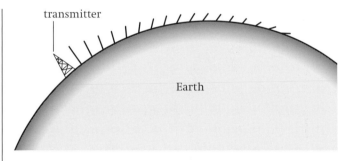

● **Figure 7.1** Surface-wave propagation.

Surface waves

In the VLF, LF and MF wavebands (i.e. for frequencies below 3 MHz), radio waves have relatively large wavelengths, up to hundreds of kilometres. Such **surface waves** tend to follow the curvature of the Earth by diffraction. These lower-frequency waves are generated by vertical aerials, as they have to be vertically polarised (in horizontal polarisation the low-resistance Earth would short-circuit the electric component of the waves, so that they would not travel very far). Such waves are affected by the conductivity of the Earth, and this causes the waves to tilt forward, as shown in *figure 7.1*.

Because they bend round the Earth's surface, these waves will propagate well beyond the visual horizon of the transmitter. How far they propagate is a function of the power of the transmitter, the frequency of the waves and the conductivity of the surface over which they pass. In the VLF and LF wavebands (i.e. between 3 kHz and 300 kHz), with a high-power transmitter, they will travel for thousands of kilometres and can be used for worldwide communications such as ship-to-shore telegraphy or long-range navigation. In the MF waveband, however, their range is much reduced and they will only propagate distances of the order of hundreds of kilometres. This fact is useful for AM sound broadcasting, because countries that are not near neighbours can use the same MF frequencies.

Note that in some textbooks, the surface wave may be referred to as a **ground wave**, although this is not strictly correct as the wave at the ground is actually a combination of the surface wave and the space wave (see below). However, at low frequencies the surface wave is dominant, so the ground wave is effectively a surface wave.

Sky waves

In the HF waveband (i.e. frequencies from 3 MHz to 30 MHz), **sky waves** propagate over long distances by refraction in the ionosphere and reflection at the surface of the Earth. The refraction in the ionosphere results in a gradual form of total internal reflection, so that the sky wave is returned to Earth. For frequencies greater than 30 MHz, the waves manage to penetrate the ionosphere before total internal reflection occurs. The process is shown in *figure 7.2*.

For any given frequency in the HF range, there is a minimum ground distance over which communication by a sky wave can be established. This is known as the **skip distance**, and any attempt to reduce it by directing the HF waves more vertically will result in penetration of the waves through the ionosphere. This is shown in *figure 7.3*, where a HF transmitting aerial *A* directs radio waves into the atmosphere; some of this radiated power will travel by ground waves (i.e. the combined surface and space waves) and the remainder will travel by sky waves.

In the HF waveband the ground wave will be dissipated in the relatively short distance *AB*, so its maximum range will be the point *B*. The point *C* is at the minimum distance to which the sky wave can return after its first curve. The distance *AC* is the skip distance. The region between points

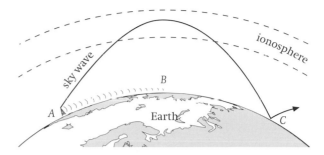

● **Figure 7.3** The sky-wave skip zone is *BC*. The ground wave is the combination of the surface and space waves.

B and *C* is a region of no reception and is called the **skip zone**. Skip distances for a single hop vary from a few hundred kilometres to about 4000 km, depending on frequency.

Any radio wave that travels in the ionosphere will be subject to some attenuation. As the state of the ionosphere varies with time, the attenuation of the radio wave and thus the signal received will also vary with time.

The sky waves that arrive at a receiving aerial will normally be composed of waves that have travelled over two or more different paths through the ionosphere. The actual signal received will therefore be the vector sum of the individual waves, which may interfere constructively or destructively. This is shown in *figure 7.4*. Again, as the state of the ionosphere varies with time then the nature of the interference will also vary with time.

Gradual variations in the received signal as a result of attenuation or interference are known as **fading** (out or in). This makes HF point-to-point communication links using space waves problematic and often unreliable. For example, in order to maintain an HF point-to-point link over long distances, the carrier frequency must be

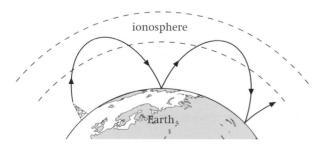

● **Figure 7.2** Sky-wave propagation.

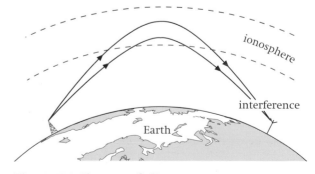

● **Figure 7.4** Sky-wave fading.

changed several times over a 24-hour period so as to coincide with ionospheric changes.

With a suitably powerful transmitter, sky waves in the HF waveband can be used for worldwide communications such as point-to-point radio telephony and AM sound broadcasting. The short-wave band (i.e. HF) on any standard radio receiver will easily pick up radio stations from around the world.

SAQ 7.1

An HF transmission is directed into the ionosphere at an angle of 30° to the horizontal. Assuming that the signal is returned to Earth by the F_1 layer at 200 km, estimate the skip distance. (Assume a flat Earth.)

Space waves

At frequencies above 30 MHz (i.e. in the VHF, UHF, SHF and EHF wavebands), the range of the surface waves is extremely small and the ionosphere does not produce any significant refraction that would return sky waves to the ground. Furthermore, the wavelength is so small that the waves tend to travel in straight lines, unlike surface waves. This straight-line propagation is known as **space-wave** or **line-of-sight** transmission and is shown in *figure 7.6*. This figure can be contrasted with *figure 7.1*.

For space-wave propagation the signal path between the transmitter and the receiver must be above the horizon, otherwise the Earth (or any hills) would block the transmission. The maximum range of space waves for terrestrial use depends on the heights of the transmitting and receiving aerials. Separations of up to 100 km can be achieved if the transmitter and receiver are sufficiently high, but this is not normal. Space waves used in broadcasting (e.g. FM radio) typically have a range from about 25 km to 40 km.

● **Figure 7.6** Space-wave propagation.

The ionosphere

The ionosphere is formed in the thin upper reaches of the Earth's atmosphere by ultraviolet radiation from the Sun. This radiation has sufficient energy to knock electrons out of the air molecules and, in so doing, to generate free electrons and positive ions. The degree of ionisation is measured by the number of free electrons per cubic metre. This number density varies with altitude. Where the atmosphere is rare, the degree of ionisation is small; nevertheless, where the atmosphere is denser there is proportionately more recombination of free electrons and positive ions.

The ionosphere is composed of four layers, each of which have different free electron densities, at heights between about 50 km and about 500 km. This is shown in *figure 7.5*. The free electron density is greatest in the F_2 layer and smallest in the D layer. Indeed, the D layer disappears at night when the ultraviolet rays disappear. The thickness and density of the other layers vary too, with both the time of day and the time of year. The ionosphere is also affected by the 11-year cycle of solar flares.

For comparison, note that at an altitude of 10 km, the air is so thin that a person could not breathe (at least, not for very long).

Note also that aeroplanes are constrained, by a balance of considerations, to fly at heights below about 20 km.

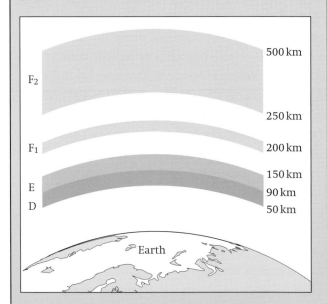

● **Figure 7.5** The layers of the ionosphere.

Broadcasting problems

Suppose that we want to set up a radio station to broadcast news and music to an entire country. Also, suppose that the country is a circular island

200 km in diameter. The questions to be asked are as follows.

■ What should be the bandwidth of the news and music information?

■ Should the carrier be modulated as AM or FM?

■ In what waveband will the carrier or carriers be located?

■ How many transmitters will be required to cover the entire country?

Solution 1

If the bandwidth of the information is limited to low fidelity (i.e. frequencies between 100 Hz to 3.5 kHz) then the most economical solution would be to use one LF or MF transmitter and amplitude-modulate the carrier with the information. The single transmitter should be positioned in the middle of the country and, because LF and MF waves propagate over long distances as surface waves, no other transmitters will be required. Thus, anywhere in the country people will be able to pick up the signal with a suitable receiver. This is shown in *figure 7.7*.

Solution 2

However, if the bandwidth of the information is to be high fidelity (i.e. frequencies between 20 Hz to 15 kHz), then frequency modulation should be used. This rules out the use of LF or MF carriers, because these wavebands cannot accommodate the large bandwidth required for FM. Frequency-modulated radio uses the VHF waveband; this allows propagation by space waves over relatively short distances (about 40 km). Thus, making simple approximations (*figure 7.8*), 21 transmitters will be required, each broadcasting the same information in order that everyone in the country can receive it.

Note that these 21 transmitters cannot use the same carrier frequency even though they are broadcasting the same information. The reason is that neighbouring transmissions would interfere with each other in any receiver that picked up two or more similar-strength signals. Thus a whole range of different carrier frequencies has to be allocated within the VHF waveband to allow a national broadcast originating from just one station. Clearly solution 2 is more complex and more

● **Figure 7.7** Nationwide coverage with LF and MF signals.

expensive, but this is the price that must be paid if there is to be national coverage of one single source of high-bandwidth information (as is required for FM radio, and TV).

SAQ 7.2

An SHF transmitter is located at a height of 100 m on top of a tower situated at point *A*. Point *B* lies at the transmission limit.

a Find the angle θ subtended at the centre of the Earth by points *A* and *B*.

b Now calculate the range over which this transmission can be picked up by a receiver on the ground. Assume a perfectly smooth Earth, of radius 6400 km. (*Hint*: arc length = radius × angle subtended.)

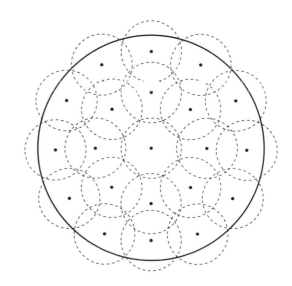

● **Figure 7.8** Nationwide coverage with VHF signals.

Basic radio receiver

All radio receivers require an aerial as the input, to convert the incoming radio waves into tiny alternating currents. As the aerial will pick up a number of different radio broadcasts at different carrier frequencies, the actual current variation in the aerial will be a complex mixture of all these signals. The receiver is designed to select one broadcast from among the many and extract its audio information. The block diagram of a basic radio receiver is shown in *figure 7.9*. The function of each block will be considered in turn.

The tuning circuit

A **tuning circuit** is essentially a **bandpass filter** in which the frequency range (i.e. the frequency band it passes) can be altered by means of a variable capacitor. The **frequency response** of the tuning circuit is the **gain** as a function of frequency, where

$$\text{gain} = \frac{\text{output voltage}}{\text{input voltage}}$$

This is shown in *figure 7.10*. If this frequency response is now superimposed on the multi-carrier signal picked up by the aerial, then we have the graph shown in *figure 7.11* (where it is assumed that all transmissions are AM). The frequency response curves for two types of tuning circuit are shown. Tuning circuit 1 has a passband that just encompasses the carrier and sidebands, and so this tuner will be very **selective**, i.e. it will pick out just one station and reject the rest. Tuning circuit 2 has a much larger passband and so is insufficiently selective; interference will occur between neighbouring transmissions.

The tuning circuit passband is centred on the desired carrier frequency and the tiny currents from this particular station are converted into

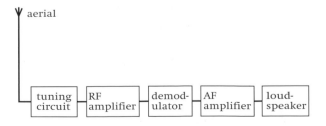

● **Figure 7.9** Block diagram of a simple radio receiver.

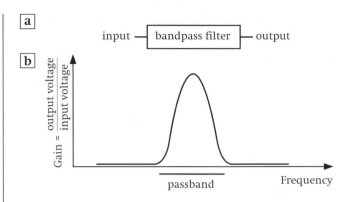

● **Figure 7.10** A tuning circuit. **a** Block diagram; **b** frequency response.

tiny voltages (typically μV or mV). Thus a tiny copy of the original AM signal will be produced.

The RF amplifier

The tiny signal voltage from the tuner might not be sufficiently large to allow the demodulator to work (in which case the radio will not work either). Consequently, the output of the tuner must be amplified by a **radio-frequency amplifier**, because the signal at this stage is still that of the radio frequency carrier. This is shown in *figure 7.12*.

Note that an RF amplifier is designed to enlarge signals that have frequencies much higher than audio frequencies. (RF may be generally taken to mean any frequency greater than 20 kHz.)

The demodulator

The **demodulator** circuit is also known as a **detector** because its function is to reject the carrier and extract (i.e. detect) the audio signal. It does this by first rectifying the AM carrier with a diode circuit, so that the average value of the AM signal is no longer zero. The half-wave rectified

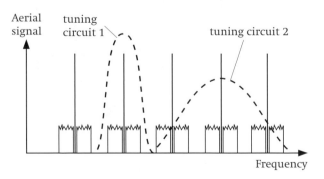

● **Figure 7.11** The frequency responses of two different tuning circuits are shown superimposed on the signal picked up by the aerial.

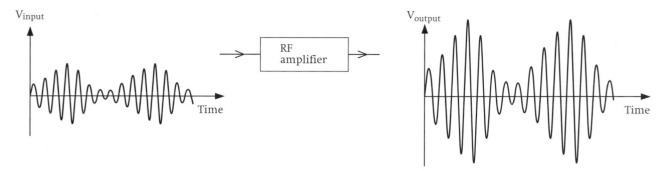

● **Figure 7.12** The action of an RF amplifier.

pulses are then smoothed with a filter, so that the carrier frequency is lost and the slowly changing envelope (i.e. the audio signal) is obtained as output. This is shown in *figure 7.13*.

Note that solid-state diodes do not allow any current through unless a signal of several hundred millivolts is applied. Thus, unless the output from the RF amplifier is at least of this order of magnitude, the diode will block the signal.

The AF amplifier

The output from the demodulator is a small audio-frequency voltage. This output voltage would be too feeble to drive a loudspeaker. The **audio-frequency amplifier** boosts the output signal in order to drive the loudspeaker. This is shown in *figure 7.14* overleaf. An AF amplifier is designed to enlarge signals at frequencies in the audio frequency range (20 to 20 kHz).

The loudspeaker

This is a transducer that converts the fluctuations in signal voltage into similar displacements of a diaphragm, so that the original audio information is recreated.

Complications

It should be noted that the radio receiver shown in *figure 7.9* simply illustrates the principles behind the recovery of audio information from an AM carrier wave. Real radio receivers are more complex than this, for the following reasons.

- Amplifiers at radio frequencies are more difficult to build, are less efficient and have a lower gain than amplifiers at lower frequencies.
  - They have to be composed of several stages, each of which should have the same passband for efficient signal transfer.
  - A radio based on *figure 7.9* would be called a tuned radio frequency (TRF) receiver, because it would require each of its RF amplifier stages to be retuned together each time it was desired to change to another station. This would require changing several controls at the same time, which the average user would find both troublesome and tedious.

These difficulties are overcome in the superheterodyne receiver; more details of this can be found in the electronics texts cited in the Bibliography.

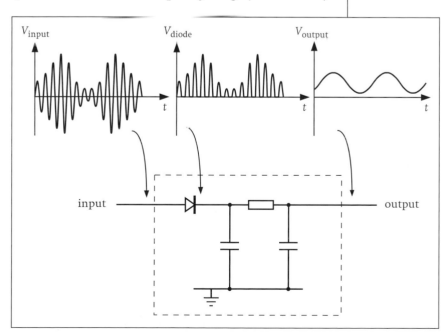

● **Figure 7.13** The action of an AM demodulator.

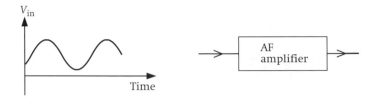

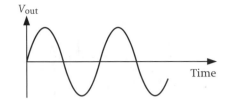

● **Figure 7.14** The action of an AF amplifier.

SUMMARY

◆ VLF and LF radio waves propagate by surface waves, which bend round the Earth's surface, for thousands of kilometres.

◆ MF radio waves propagate by surface waves for hundreds of kilometres.

◆ HF radio waves propagate by sky waves for thousands of kilometres.

◆ Sky waves undergo total internal reflection in the ionosphere, which is a series of charged layers in the upper atmosphere.

◆ Sky waves are very susceptible to fading.

◆ Space waves, also called line-of-sight waves, travel in straight lines.

◆ Radio waves at frequencies higher than 30 MHz propagate as space waves.

◆ AM broadcasts in the LF and MF wavebands are very economical.

◆ FM broadcasts require multiple transmitters operating at different frequencies, to avoid interference.

◆ A radio receiver is composed of basic building blocks. It has a tuning circuit to isolate the desired modulated carrier signal, an RF amplifier, and a demodulator to remove the carrier frequency and extract the audio signal, which is fed via an AF amplifier to the loudspeaker.

Questions

1 A large hemispherical hill is situated 20 km from a 100 kHz amplitude-modulated transmitter and 20 km from a 100 MHz FM transmitter. Explain why the AM signal can be picked up all the way around the base of the hill but the FM signal cannot.

2 In 1927, it became possible to make a telephone call from the UK to the USA, despite there not being a suitable cable under the Atlantic. The stretch across the ocean was carried by radio waves. Suggest what waveband(s) could have been used for the carrier and whether the signal crossed the ocean by surface, sky or space waves.

3 Suggest why it is not possible to pick up a French television station in London, when it *is* possible to pick up a French radio station.

4 Make a rough estimate of the number of terrestrial transmitters required to cover the USA with broadcasts from a single national TV station. (Assume the country is a rectangular shape approximately 3000 km by 2000 km and then find the radius of a circle of the same area.)

5 What is another name for a detector in an AM radio receiver and how does it work?

CHAPTER 8

Satellite systems

By the end of this chapter you should be able to:

1 understand the physics of *satellite* motion;

2 appreciate the advantages to society of using satellites;

3 understand the behaviour and uses of *polar orbiting* satellites;

4 understand the behaviour and uses of *geostationary* satellites;

5 describe the use of geostationary satellites in radio communication;

6 understand how the *global positioning system* operates.

Introduction

The physics of satellite motion has been understood since 1687, when Isaac Newton first explained why a heavenly body (such as the Moon) could orbit another body (such as the Earth) without using a fuel supply or falling down.

It was not until 1957, however, some 270 years later, that the technology of the day allowed the use of this knowledge to practical effect. The Russian Sputnik satellite astonished the world because it was the first non-heavenly body in history to orbit the Earth.

The 1957 Sputnik did not do anything other than transmit a radio signal to notify anyone with a receiver, a few hundred kilometres below, that it was passing overhead. There was no control mechanism on the satellite, nor was it possible for it to receive any signals from Earth. Each orbit lasted for about 90 minutes; the satellite transmitted for 92 days before burning up in the atmosphere.

Since 1957, of course, rocket technology and solid-state electronics have moved on apace and modern satellites can now be launched into any desired orbit and be made to perform a number of different operations, which can be broadly categorised as follows:

- monitoring some aspect of the planet below;
- radiating a signal for positioning (as in the GPS system);
- acting as a relay for long-distance point-to-point communications;
- broadcasting high-bandwidth radio and TV signals.

It is important to note that using satellites, the above four operations can be carried out very much more effectively than in the days before satellite technology existed. This effectiveness is what justifies the enormous cost and risk involved in building and launching a satellite.

Power and control

Most satellites use batteries charged from solar cells. These are not very efficient converters of light into electrical energy, so there has to be a large area of cells if the satellite requires a significant amount of power (especially so in a broadcasting satellite). Some satellites are large spin-stabilised cylinders about 3 m in diameter, with solar cells all around the outside of the cylinder. Others have their solar cells on extended arms, or wings, which can have a span of as much as 20 metres. Such appendages can produce power of the order of kilowatts.

SAQ 8.1

A satellite has a transmitter that requires 50 W from its power supply. The power supply is composed of a battery fed by solar cells. When the cells are in sunlight, they need to provide 100 W to charge the battery. If the solar cells have an efficiency of 5% and the intensity of sunlight is 1500 W m^{-2}, calculate the area of solar cells required.

Satellite motion around the Earth

Let us suppose that a satellite of mass m is placed in an orbit of radius r around the Earth, of mass M. Let us say that the linear speed in the orbit is v and the time for one orbit is T. The orbit is shown in *figure 8.1*.

The only force acting on the satellite is the gravitational force, GmM/r^2 and this force provides the **centripetal force** mv^2/r needed to keep the mass in orbit.

$$\frac{GmM}{r^2} = \frac{mv^2}{r}$$

Rearranging to make v the subject, we obtain

$$v = \sqrt{GM/r}$$

The period of orbit T of the satellite is given by

$$T = \frac{\text{circumference of orbit}}{\text{speed}}$$
$$= \frac{2\pi r}{v}$$
$$= \frac{2\pi r^{3/2}}{\sqrt{GM}}$$

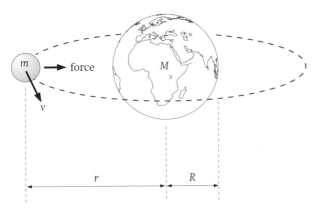

● **Figure 8.1** Satellite motion around the earth.

We can draw the following important conclusions.

- The speed required for the satellite to follow a particular orbit is independent of its mass.
- Both speed and time period depend only on the radius of orbit.
- For larger orbits the speed is less, i.e. $v \propto 1\sqrt{r}$.
- For larger orbits the period is greater, i.e. $T \propto r^{3/2}$.
- The shortest possible period, which occurs for the lowest possible orbit, when $r = R$, is 85 minutes (although this could not be achieved owing to atmospheric drag).
- The speed in the lowest possible orbit is approximately 8 km s^{-1}.

SAQ 8.2

Calculate the required speed and orbital period for a satellite to orbit at a height of 1200 km above the Earth; the radius of the Earth is 6400 km, its mass M is 6.0×10^{24} kg and G is 6.7×10^{-11} N m^2 kg^{-2}. Give the speed in km s^{-1}, km h^{-1} and miles per hour (approximately).

Many satellites have a mass in excess of one tonne and this can present huge problems if they go into an uncontrollable tumble or spin (some satellites have become unusable because of this). Thus, all satellites incorporate some form of **gyroscope** system (i.e. internal spinning flywheels) which can be adjusted for stability, and they also have small gas thruster jets for fine positioning. Indeed, control signals are regularly sent from Earth to many satellites to keep them in the required position, and this is particularly so with broadcasting satellites, where a shift of one degree could mean a total loss of signal. The gas thruster jets can also be used at the end of the satellite's useful life to push it out of its orbit and allow it (eventually) to spiral slowly downwards and be destroyed in the Earth's atmosphere.

A satellite is designed to perform a particular operation, or operations, and this will dictate the nature of its orbit. Although there are an infinite number of possible orbital distances and orbital planes, the two most commonly used are the polar orbit and the geostationary orbit.

Polar orbiting satellites

Polar orbiting satellites have a **low Earth orbit** that passes over both poles. Their height is usually of the order of hundreds of kilometres (*figure 8.2*). Note that if the orbit passes over one pole then it must pass over the other; furthermore, any such low-orbiting satellite will have an orbital period of about 100 minutes and a speed of about 7.5 km s^{-1}.

Underneath a polar orbiting satellite, the Earth is slowly rotating with a period of 24 hours. Thus, sooner or later, the satellite will pass over every area on Earth. This makes such satellites ideal for **remote sensing**. Some examples are as follows:

- military reconnaissance;
- meteorology;
- oceanography;
- cartography;
- geological prospecting.

In all these operations the satellite picks up information from below and stores it. As it passes over the appropriate receiver, the information is downloaded.

Low-Earth-orbiting satellites can also be used for the communication of messages: a message can be sent from a transmitter to the satellite as it is passing overhead. The satellite stores this message in its memory. Later, while it is passing over a different location, the message is transmitted down to a receiver.

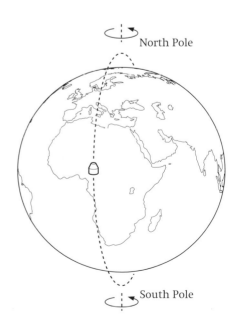

● **Figure 8.2** A polar orbit.

Communicating with a low-Earth-orbiting satellite sometimes involves using tracking aerials to follow it as it moves across the sky. To a fixed observer, not near the poles, the satellite will only be in view for about 10 minutes at a time, twice per day. For an observer at or near the poles, however, the satellite will be in view every 100 minutes or so, and such satellites are used to communicate with the polar regions, where geostationary satellite signals (see below) cannot be picked up. The frequencies used to communicate with and transmit from polar orbiting satellites range from about 150 MHz to several GHz. The lifetime of these satellites is usually estimated to be about five years.

Worked example

Suppose a polar orbiting satellite is launched into an orbit with a height of 600 km. It will then have an orbital radius of $r = 6400 + 600 = 7000$ km. Using the values of M and G from SAQ 8.2, the orbital time period T and orbital speed v will then be given by

$$T = 2\pi r^{3/2}/\sqrt{GM} = 97 \text{ minutes}$$

$$v = \sqrt{GM/r} = 7.56 \text{ km s}^{-1}$$

A diagram of this orbit is shown in *figure 8.3*. Each time the satellite crosses the equator, the Earth will have rotated west by a certain angle since the satellite's previous orbit.

a What is this angle?

b What is the corresponding equatorial displacement?

c For how long is the satellite in view to an observer on the equator?

a Remember that in 24 hours the Earth rotates by 360°. Thus in 97 minutes

$$\text{angular rotation} = \frac{97}{24 \times 60} \times 360°$$
$$= 24.25° \text{ due west}$$

b The total displacement of a point on the equator over 24 hours is the Earth's circumference, $2\pi R$, where $R = 6400$ km. Thus in 97 minutes we have

$$\text{equatorial displacement} = \frac{97}{24 \times 60} \times 2\pi R$$
$$= 2700 \text{ km}$$

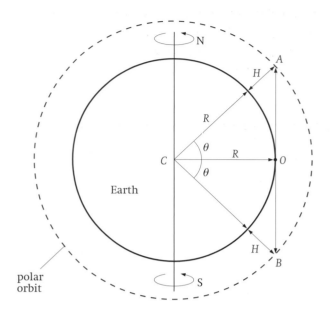

● **Figure 8.3** The path of communication with a polar orbit is the arc AB, where points A and B lie in opposite directions on the horizon of observer O.

c We assume a perfectly smooth Earth surface. To find out how long the satellite will be in view to (and therefore be communicable with) an observer at a fixed position on the ground, we use *figure 8.3*, where A and B show the satellite at the observer O's horizon. We can now ignore the relatively slow rotation of the Earth and simply ask, what is the angle 2θ subtended at the centre of the Earth by the arc AB? We use the right-angled triangle COA:

$$\cos\theta = \frac{R}{R+H} = \frac{6400}{7000} = 0.914$$

Thus

$$\theta = 23.9°$$

So the total angle subtended during the satellite pass $= 2 \times 23.9° = 47.8°$, and the time for which the satellite is in view $= \dfrac{47.8}{360} \times 97 \approx 13$ minutes.

Geostationary satellites

In 1945, the science fiction writer Arthur C. Clarke wrote an article entitled 'Extra-terrestrial relays' for the magazine *Wireless World*. In this article he suggested that if satellites could be launched into a geosynchronous (i.e. geostationary) orbit then they could be used as relays with repeater amplifiers for any radio signals directed at them. However, the various technologies needed to realise such an idea were not then available. Eventually, in 1965, the first commercial communications satellite, Intelsat 1, called *Early Bird*, was launched.

For a satellite to be in a geostationary orbit, three conditions have to be satisfied.

■ The period of orbit must be the same as that of the Earth's rotation, i.e. 24 hours.

■ The satellite must orbit directly above the equator.

■ It must rotate in the same sense as the Earth.

If these conditions are met, then the satellite will appear to remain fixed in the sky relative to any point on Earth. A diagram of a geostationary orbit is shown in *figure 8.4*.

It is essential that the satellite is positioned directly above the equator, because the axis of the orbit must be the spin axis of the Earth. Thus, in the northern hemisphere all geostationary satellites appear in the southern sky while in the southern hemisphere all geostationary satellites appear in the northern sky.

The radius of orbit of a geostationary satellite is determined by the requirement that its time period in 24 hours; it is approximately 42 000 km. This makes its height above the equator equal to 42 000 − 6400 ≈ 36 000 km. To communicate with such a satellite, the signal must be propagated through an enormous distance. This places severe restrictions on the carrier frequencies that can be used for the link, as explained below.

Low, medium and high frequencies (*table 6.1* on page 46) could not be used because:

■ these waves have difficulty penetrating the ionosphere (see chapter 7);

● **Figure 8.4** A geostationary orbit.

- they cannot be focussed into a beam easily;

- the signal received at a small satellite would be lost in the noise;

- they cannot carry a large enough bandwidth to justify the expense of installation and use.

Very high frequencies (*table 6.1*) are not used because:

- although they could be focussed in space using huge parabolic dishes, the dish would be too large to be launched with a satellite;

- the inevitable diffraction spread from a transmitter would still severely limit the signal strength received;

- the information-carrying capacity is still not large enough to justify the expense.

The wavebands used for communication with geostationary satellites are thus the UHF and SHF wavebands. In these wavebands the wavelengths are of the order of centimetres. They are used because:

- very small wavelengths are relatively easy to focus into a parallel beam;

- a huge bandwidth is available, so a large number of separate signals can be multiplexed together;

- for UH and SH frequencies, a relatively large power can be produced by relatively low-amplitude waves (wave power $\propto$ square of amplitude).

It is more or less essential to use parabolic dish aerials with geostationary satellites because there can be as much as 200 dB signal loss between the transmitter on Earth and the receiver on the satellite. (Remember, a 200 dB loss means the ratio of signal received to signal sent is 10^{-20}!) As explained in chapter 6, a parabolic dish allows a highly directional and powerful signal to be transmitted and a stronger signal to be received.

Use of geostationary satellites

A geostationary satellite may be used for three basic purposes.

- **As a weather monitor**
  Although the satellite is high above the Earth, it has a permanent, uninterrupted, full view of one third of the Earth's surface and can thus be used for continuous monitoring of changes in climatic conditions and long-term weather predictions.

- **As a microwave link**
  Using such a satellite, microwave signals can be sent from a transmitter T at a **ground station** to a receiver R at a different place, as if there were a huge-bandwidth cable stretching into the sky, up to the satellite and back again. This is shown in *figure 8.5*; the two points, T and R, could be many thousands of kilometres apart.

- **For broadcasting high-bandwidth signals over a large area**
  In this mode, the information source, say a TV station, transmits a highly focussed powerful beam towards the satellite. The satellite picks up this transmission and then transmits it back to Earth in a somewhat less focussed beam (*figure 8.6*). In this way, a huge area can be covered with high-bandwidth signals by a *single* transmitter (i.e. the satellite). It should be noted that it would require thousands of transmitters to cover the same area with terrestrial aerials

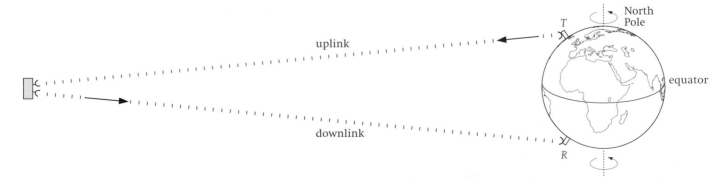

● **Figure 8.5** A geostationary satellite can be used as a microwave link for communications.

(see chapter 7). The area covered by the broadcast from the satellite is referred to as its **footprint**; this area can be made large or small by suitable design of the dish aerial.

Transponders

All geostationary satellites carry several **transponders**. A transponder can both transmit and respond and is essentially composed of three circuits:

■ a **tuned receiver**, with a 40 MHz passband, to accept a carrier signal from the ground station (this signal is of very low power by the time it arrives);

■ a **frequency changer** to shift the carrier to a new frequency;

■ a **power amplifier** to boost the new signal before it is returned to Earth.

The frequency changer is necessary because of the possibility of positive feedback (see chapter 12) between the sensitive receiver (which will pick up tiny signals) and the relatively powerful transmitter. If they operated at the same frequency then oscillation could result, so that the input signal would be swamped by the output (this is what gives the screeching sound feedback between microphone and loudspeaker in a hall). The frequency changer does not have any effect on the modulated signal.

Modern transponders can now double their use if the carrier frequency is arranged to have both vertical and horizontal polarisations (these two differently polarised signals will not interfere), so that two carriers are created from one. For example, the six ASTRA satellites, which provide most of the satellite TV for the UK and which have eight transponders per satellite, can each broadcast 16 different TV channels.

Frequencies and modulation

The path from the ground station to the satellite is called the **uplink** and the return path is known as the **downlink** (*figure 8.5*). Uplink carrier frequencies are by convention always arranged to be higher than downlink carrier frequencies; typical bands and bandwidth are shown in *table 8.1*.

Most of the modulation techniques available for terrestrial communications have been used with satellite communications. Some use analogue forms and some use digital. For example, the ASTRA satellites receive and broadcast using carriers (in the 14 GHz/11 GHz range) modulated by FM, each TV station being allocated a bandwidth of approximately 30 MHz. The new ASTRA 2 satellite, however, is digital and thus uses time-division multiplexing (see chapter 6) to accommodate a large number of different channels. In the future, almost all satellite communication will be digital.

Uplink (GHz)	Downlink (GHz)	Bandwidth (MHz)
6	4	500
14	11	500
30	20	1500

● **Table 8.1** Uplink and downlink frequencies with their corresponding bandwidths.

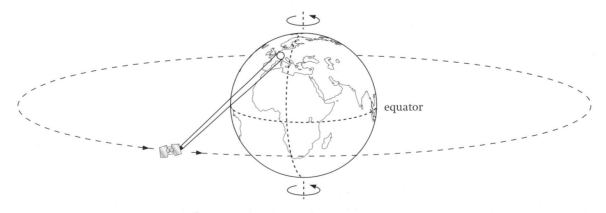

● **Figure 8.6** A geostationary satellite broadcasting to a specific area. The footprint of this transmission beam covers central Europe.

Intelsat

The International Satellite Telecommunications Organisation (Intelsat) was formed in 1964 by 11 countries, as a non-profit cooperative to provide global coverage for users of telecommunications services. It meant shared costs for the enormous expense of launching communications satellites into orbit. Since its formation, the organisation has expanded to include most of the countries in the world and now relatively few countries actually own their own satellites.

If a telecommunications company or organisation decides to launch a geostationary satellite, it will be assigned an orbit position and a frequency band in which to operate. For example, the six ASTRA satellites are located in a 70 km cube at a position 28° west of south. Each satellite is allocated particular carrier frequencies within the frequency band for the group and, as mentioned above, each frequency is used twice. The total bandwidth available to each satellite depends on the allocated frequency band.

Ground stations transmitting to geostationary satellites can use transmission powers of the order of kilowatts but the satellite itself is only able to transmit signal powers up to about 30 W, if low- or medium-powered, or about 300 W if high-powered.

The lifetime of geostationary satellites is usually estimated to be about 15 years.

Looking south from the UK

If you looked towards the south from the UK and could see all those satellites in geostationary orbit around the equator (remember, they are 36 000 km away) then those visible in your field of view would appear as the dots in *figure 8.7*. With a steerable parabolic dish and the appropriate receivers, you have a massive source of information on your doorstep.

SAQ 8.3

Calculate the angular limits in latitude, relative to the equator, within which the signals from a geostationary satellite can be picked up. The radius R of the Earth is 6400 km and the radius of orbit of the satellite is 42 000 km. (Hint. Sketch the Earth and the satellite S and draw tangents from S to the Earth. The points where the tangents meet the Earth define the northern and southern limits between which the signals can be picked up.)

Global positioning system (GPS)

The **global positioning system** (GPS) was originally developed for military use in the United States. It is a worldwide navigation system which allows users to locate their positions on Earth with remarkable accuracy. The system is composed of 24 satellites, positioned in six different orbits. Within each orbit there are four satellites. The six orbits are all at the same 20 000 km height but are in different planes. The six orbital planes are spaced 60° apart and inclined at about 55° to the equatorial plane. The arrangement is shown in *figure 8.8*.

The satellites are all moving with the same orbital period of almost 12 hours, so each satellite

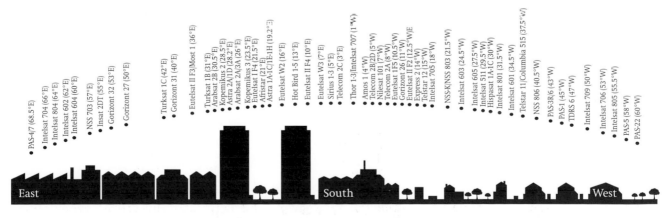

● **Figure 8.7** TV geostationary satellites looking south from the UK.

covers almost the same track round the Earth twice per day. As one disappears out of the field of view, another will appear. The 24 satellites are so spaced that any observer, at any time and at any place, will be able to see a minimum of six satellites.

The system is controlled from the Schriever Air Force Base in Colorado. This master control station and four other monitoring stations situated at different locations on Earth are constantly tracking the satellites and updating the information to be transmitted from them. In this way, each satellite knows its exact position, and it transmits this information as a digital signal back to Earth; the carrier frequencies used are around 1.5 GHz.

● **Figure 8.8** The global positioning system (GPS). There are 24 GPS satellites, each occupying one of six different orbits.

At the same time, the satellite transmits the time signal of an atomic clock accurate to one second in 70 000 years. Now, each GPS receiver also has a very accurate clock, and if the GPS receiver and the GPS satellite were located next to each other then the two clocks would agree.

The GPS receiver is programmed to compare its internal clock with that transmitted by the satellite; the comparison will yield the time taken for the satellite signal to reach the receiver and this will be of the order of 0.1 second (remember, radio waves travel at the speed of light). Through this calculation, the receiver determines the distance from the receiver to the particular satellite.

At any time, as mentioned above, there are six satellites in view; the receiver calculates the distances to four of them and these four distances are used to define the receiver's position in terms of latitude, longitude and altitude.

Following the end of the cold war, the GPS system was made available for public use. Receivers are now mounted in aircraft, ships and even cars, which can thus determine their position with an accuracy that depends on the electronic sophistication of the receiver. Low-cost receivers provide a 100 metre accuracy, while high-cost receivers allow the user to pinpoint their position to the nearest centimetre.

Portable receivers are also available (they are about the size of a mobile phone) and these have proved an invaluable asset for mountaineers and trekkers all over the world.

SUMMARY

◆ Satellites allow efficient and fast monitoring of the planet. They act as a relay point in the sky to increase the range of space waves.

◆ A single satellite can broadcast several high-bandwidth signals to a huge area.

◆ All satellites require solar cells and stability control.

◆ Polar orbiting satellites are in a low Earth orbit and see everywhere twice daily. They are ideal for remote sensing.

◆ Communication with a polar orbiting satellite lasts about ten minutes.

◆ For a satellite to be in a geostationary orbit, three conditions must be satisfied: its period must be 24 hours, its orbit must lie above the equator and its direction must be that of the Earth's rotation.

◆ Geostationary satellites contain transponders, use the UHF and SHF wavebands, require parabolic-dish transmitting and receiving aerials, have a period of 24 hours, and have several channels of communication.

Questions

1 A low-Earth-orbit satellite transmits weather data twice daily to a receiving station in northern Scotland using a carrier of 150 MHz. Suggest why this satellite does not require a large area of solar cells and why the receiving aerial is a Yagi array (see chapter 6).

2 A geostationary satellite broadcasts a 250 W TV signal over a circular footprint 700 km in diameter. Assuming all the power is contained in this footprint, calculate the maximum power received on Earth by a dish of diameter 1.5 metres.

3 A ground station transmits a signal power of 1.8 kW towards a geostationary satellite. If there is a 180 dB loss in the uplink, calculate the signal power actually received by the satellite.

4 A telephone call is made from London to New York via a geostationary satellite. Estimate the transit time for the signal to travel between the two callers.

5 Suggest why long-distance telephone calls never involve more than one geostationary satellite link.

CHAPTER 9

The telephone system

By the end of this chapter you should be able to:

1 understand how the *public switched telephone network* (PSTN) developed;

2 understand how a telephone handset communicates with the local exchange;

3 appreciate the role of *switching* in a modern telecommunications network;

4 understand how *multiplexing* in the PSTN operates and why it is necessary;

5 recall that information may be carried by a number of different *channels*, including wire-pairs, coaxial cables, radio and microwave links and optic fibres;

6 demonstrate that a modern telecommunications system links together different channels of communication, depending upon location, distance and required bandwidth;

7 estimate and use typical power levels and attenuations associated with different channels of communication;

8 discuss the relative advantages and disadvantages of channels of communication in terms of available bandwidth, noise, cross-linking, security, signal attenuation, regeneration, cost and convenience;

9 explain the principles of operation of a cellular mobile telephone network.

The public switched telephone network (PSTN)

When telephones were first introduced, each user was connected directly to every other user by their own cable. This involved considerable wiring and was only viable for a relatively small number of users within a single building. Such an arrangement for five users is shown in *figure 9.1*, where it can be seen that 10 connecting cables are required.

Once it was realised that the telephone could be used for communication over longer distances, the **telephone exchange** was invented. Thus instead of each user calling any other user directly, as in *figure 9.1*, he or she had to call the exchange, which made the connection. This is shown in *figure 9.2*, where it should be noted that only five cables are used.

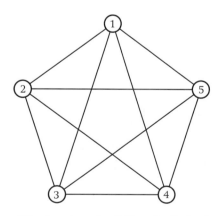

● **Figure 9.1** A network of directly linked telephones.

As the system expanded, the exchange in one town became wired to the exchange in another town through what became known as a **trunk line** (*figure 9.3*). Thus calls became distinguished by being either local calls (e.g. user 3 calling user 5) or trunk calls (e.g. user 2 calling user 9). Trunk

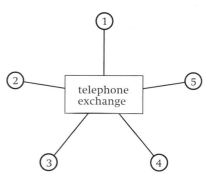

● **Figure 9.2** A network that uses a telephone exchange.

calls were more expensive because these lines were not dedicated to any one user and, until multiplexing was developed, the line was tied up for as long as two people wished to use it.

As the system expanded still further, trunk exchanges became necessary, to link groups of local exchanges together. Then international exchanges appeared, until the entire planet was covered in a mesh of cables capable of connecting any two telephones anywhere on Earth.

At first, all exchanges were operated manually, by people who became known as *operators*. As the technology improved, however, the operators were replaced, initially with slow and unreliable electromechanical switches and then with fast, reliable electronic systems with no moving parts. The last public manual exchange in the UK closed in 1976. Note that, in the UK, 90% of all users live within 3 km of their local exchange, of which there are over 600. There are about 60 trunk exchanges.

If a phone call is not a local call, then the local exchange passes all the dialled information to a trunk exchange. If the phone call is not destined for a user who is local to that trunk then it is passed to the appropriate trunk. If the call is an international call, then it is passed from the trunk to an international **gateway** (*figure 9.4*). A gateway is an electronic device that interconnects incompatible networks by performing protocol conversions. Protocols are explained in chapter 11.

The telephone circuit

Figure 9.5 shows the basic circuit by which telephones operate. Once the exchange has made the link between user 1 and user 2 there is a symmetrical set up, so it does not matter who speaks and who listens or if both activities are engaged in together. A system that allows the simultaneous, two-way flow of information is said to be **full-duplex**. In a **half-duplex** system information can flow in both directions but not at the same time (e.g. systems with a switch to transmit or receive). An exclusively one-way transmission system is called **simplex**.

In the duplex system of *figure 9.5*, the exchange battery powers the line through an inductor L (i.e. a coil of wire wound round a soft iron core). When user 1 speaks, the result will be a changing current in the handset of user 2. This current will be in the same direction for both primary coils P_2 and therefore the changing magnetic flux of both of these coils will add and generate a large induced e.m.f. in the secondary S_2. This induced e.m.f. drives the earphone of user 2. The changing current is also applied to user 1's transformer. However, the changing current is *not* in the same direction in the two primary coils P_1 and so the magnetic flux generated by these two coils tends to cancel. Thus there is almost no e.m.f. generated in user 1's own secondary S_1. This eliminates the disturbing effect called **sidetone**, when you hear yourself in your own earphone; this echoing effect

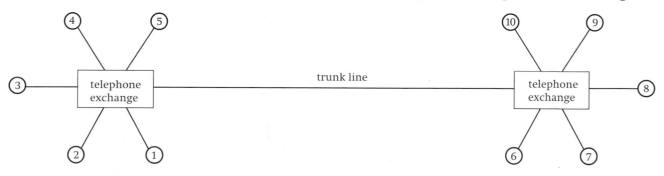

● **Figure 9.3** A trunk line linking two exchanges.

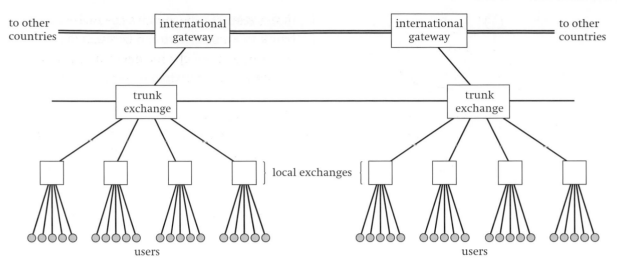

● **Figure 9.4** International telephone communications. The squares above the users indicate the local exchanges.

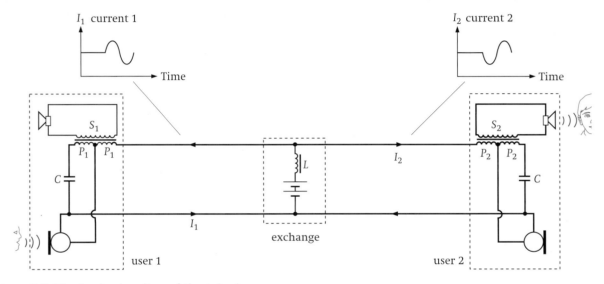

● **Figure 9.5** The basic circuitry of the telephone system connecting two users.

causes you to lower your voice, because it sounds so loud in your ear.

Dialling a number

Until the 1970s, local telephone exchanges were still largely electromechanical, in other words they had systems with moving parts. Mechanical movement takes a significant time to change position; thus early telephone dials were deliberately organised to be slow, so as to output the same number of current pulses into the line as the number from which the finger had started. These current pulses caused an array of selector switches to shift position by whatever number had been dialled. This system was known as **pulse dialling**.

Once telephone exchanges became entirely electronic (i.e. they no longer had moving parts), there was no need to delay the progression of numbers along the line. Consequently, a new method of dialling was developed, using push-buttons and audio frequency tones to communicate the desired number. Each number on the phone generates two identifying frequencies from a group of eight separate pure tones. The frequencies have to be in the range 300 Hz to 3.4 kHz, because this is the range to which the telephone is restricted (as explained in chapter 2). *Figure 9.6* shows a typical phone keypad with the numbers arranged in a matrix.

■ If key 1 is pushed then the two frequencies 687 Hz and 1209 Hz are generated.

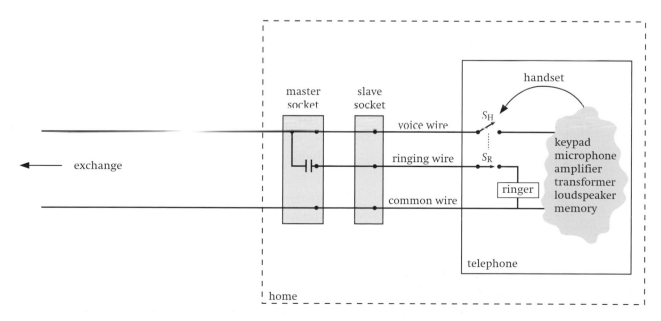

high group

1209 1336 1477 1633 Hz

	1209	1336	1477	1633
687	1	2	3	A
770	4	5	6	B
852	7	8	9	C
941	*	0	#	D

low group

Hz

● **Figure 9.6** A modern telephone dual-tone multi-frequency (DTMF) keypad.

■ If key 5 is pushed then the two frequencies 770 Hz and 1336 Hz are generated.

■ If key 9 is pushed then the two frequencies 852 Hz and 1477 Hz are generated.

The pair of tones is generated and the two tones are then combined by dedicated circuits inside the phone and sent down the telephone line to the exchange, where special filter circuits are able to identify the signal as a number code and not a human voice. The tone frequencies were chosen to be non-harmonically related, so that they cannot be mimicked by the voice (you might be able to whistle a note of frequency, say, 687 Hz, but you would not be able to whistle 1209 Hz at the same time).

This system of dialling is called **dual-tone multifrequency** (DTMF) but is also known as touch-tone or tone dialling. It is faster and more reliable than pulse dialling and has the further advantage that the pairs of tones can be used for communicating telephone numbers throughout the analogue (i.e. audio frequency) part of the network.

SAQ 9.1
When you press key 3 on a DTMF telephone, what two frequencies are generated?

The ringing wire

The line from the exchange to the home is simply a pair of wires terminating in a master socket. The master-socket output consists of three wires: a voice wire, a ringing wire and a common wire. This is shown in *figure 9.7*. Inside the telephone there are two switches:

■ S_H is normally open but *closes* when the handset is lifted from its cradle (or hook);

■ S_R is normally closed but *opens* when the handset is lifted from its cradle.

When an incoming call is to be received, the exchange sends voltage pulses down the line; these pass through the capacitor (remember, a capacitor allows a.c. to flow) and through the switch S_R to the ringer, which is then activated. Note that these voltage pulses normally fluctuate between 0 V and 50 V.

When the user picks up the handset, switch S_R opens (this disconnects the ringer) and switch S_H closes (this completes the d.c. link with the caller).

● **Figure 9.7** The ringing circuit arrangement.

The capacitor prevents any d.c. current from the exchange entering the ringer while the handset is in its resting position.

Many homes now have slave sockets into which extension phones can be plugged. These allow the additional phones to be wired in parallel, so that the incoming exchange pulses will activate all the ringers of the phones at the same time.

SAQ 9.2

When a handset is picked up following the activation of the ringer, the exchange stops sending voltage pulses down the line. Suggest how the exchange knew that the user had picked up the handset.

The telephone exchange: switching

Cross-point switching

Some telephone exchanges are operated using the principles of **cross-point switching**, in which the various users' lines are formed into a matrix of wires at right angles to each other (*figure 9.8*). Where the wires cross there is a switch, which is electronic, not electromechanical. If this switch is closed then those two users are connected. *Figure 9.8* shows the basic arrangement for six users.

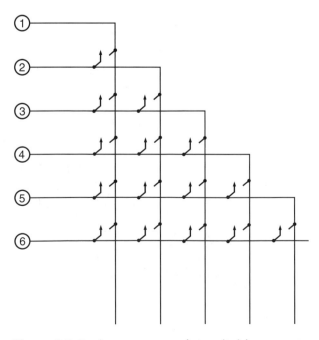

● **Figure 9.8** Exchange cross-point switching.

Note that in this system of six users there are 15 switches; however, only three of them would ever be closed at any one time because there could never be more than three phone calls going on among the six users. Thus most of these switches are unused for most of the time. This is very inefficient: if there are N users, there would be a total of $\frac{1}{2}N(N-1)$ switches and if N is large (there can be 10 000 users at an exchange) then an enormous number of switches would have been installed to do mostly nothing.

Time-slot switching

Modern exchanges are operated on the principle of **time-slot switching**, which works as follows. The two wires from each user's telephone feed into a local exchange, known as a **concentrator unit**, which converts the call from analogue into digital (*figure 9.9*). The concentrator unit is linked to a **digital call centre exchange**, which controls the local area. This is essentially a memory-based system: the digitised samples of each call are allocated time slots in a huge memory and then directed to an appropriate destination (i.e. either to another local user or into the trunk network).

Thus, even if you telephone your next-door neighbour, your conversation will be broken up into digitised samples, the samples will be held for a few moments in a memory, then extracted from the memory and finally converted back to analogue. Digital call centre exchanges are linked by trunk cables to **digital main switching units**, which control the traffic on the main network. There are about 60 main switching units in the UK.

Transporting telephone signals

Copper wires

The original system for transporting telephone signals was via current-carrying copper wires supported by telegraph poles. These poles were made to carry several open wires (and thus to carry several phone calls) and were designed to keep each wire as far away from any other as was practical. The reason was that the changing current in one wire causes radiation to others, which results in serious crosstalk. This system is shown in *figure 9.10*.

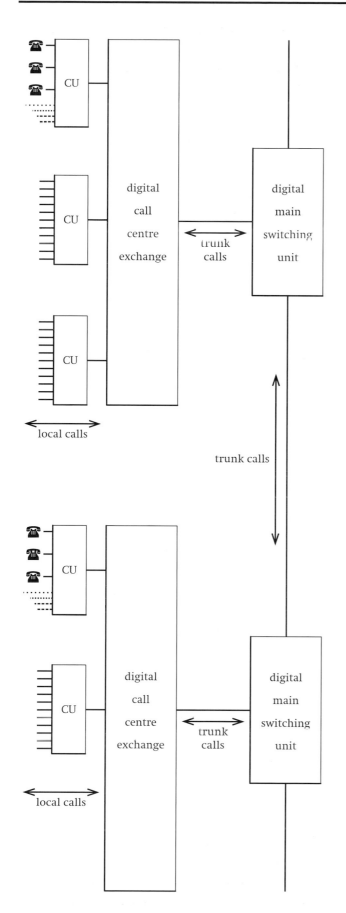

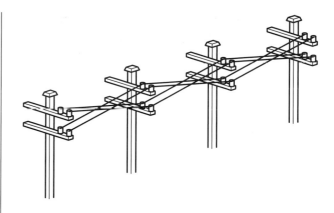

● **Figure 9.10** Open wires on telegraph poles.

Wire-pairs

A later development was to insulate each copper
wire and then twist two of these wires together.
The resulting twisted pair of wires was then
further insulated by an outer covering of insulation
to form a **cable**. In telecommunications, this
double-insulated, twisted arrangement is known as
an **unscreened twisted pair** (UTP) or, simply, a
wire-pair. Crosstalk is reduced, because at any
moment in time the current in one wire will be in
the opposite direction to the current in the other,
so their magnetic fields will tend to cancel. A two-
wire cable is shown in *figure 9.11*, although it
should be noted that cables that enclose several
pairs twisted together are often used.

Coaxial cable

As the frequencies used in telecommunications
increased, wire-pairs became more and more
inefficient: with increasing frequency, the
attenuation of the signal in the wire-pair becomes
higher and higher, crosstalk becomes more of a

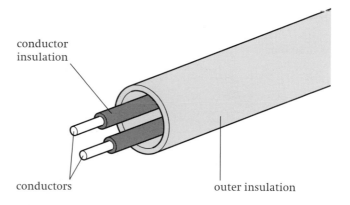

conductor
insulation

conductors

outer insulation

● **Figure 9.9** A modern digital exchange system. The
boxes labelled CU are concentrator units.

● **Figure 9.11** A wire-pair.

problem and distortion arises because different high frequencies travel at slightly different speeds. A special cable was therefore developed for use at high frequencies, and this cable has one conductor completely surrounded by the other. The cable is called **coaxial**, because the two conductors share the same axis and is shown in *figure 9.12*.

In coaxial cable, the signal is applied to the central copper conductor and the copper braid is used for the return path. Normally the braid is connected to Earth. The bandwidth of coaxial cable is much higher than for wire-pairs, and so it became widely used for the trunk network until microwave links and optic fibres appeared.

Optic fibres

Optic fibres are now replacing coaxial cable on trunk and international lines and will be discussed separately in chapter 10.

Microwave links

Although microwave links (*figure 9.13*) were first used for transporting television signals, they have been used also to carry telephone signals. Indeed, before optic fibres took over, a significant proportion of the UK's telephone trunk was carried by this system. The microwave link has three fundamental advantages over coaxial cable.

■ A microwave link is equivalent to a cable, but without the associated costs and delays of having to bury it underground.

■ Such a link is by line-of-sight, so it can be propagated uninterrupted through several tens of kilometres, whereas signals in

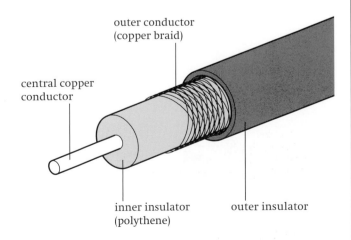

● **Figure 9.12** A coaxial cable.

● **Figure 9.13** A microwave link.

underground coaxial cable have to be amplified every few kilometres.

■ This high-frequency link has a very large bandwidth, so it can be multiplexed to carry a greater number of independent channels than coaxial cable.

Multiplexing on the telephone

Before multiplexing was developed the telephone was a relatively expensive system, especially for trunk, or long-distance, calls: while a call was in progress, anyone else was prevented from using the line. Consequently several trunk lines were laid in parallel between one exchange and another, so that the maximum number of simultaneous calls was equal to the number of lines that had been laid. This was essentially a process of **space multiplexing**. Laying more and more cables to accommodate more and more calls, however, was not an economically viable solution. The first multiplexing system (see chapter 6) used by all the early telephone companies was frequency-division multiplexing (FDM), because all the signals in the network at this time were analogue signals. Once digital technology was developed, however, there was a gradual shift to time-division multiplexing (TDM), and nowadays all the major trunk and international phone traffic travels by this system.

Frequency-division multiplexing on the telephone

In this system, each call was made to modulate an RF carrier by amplitude modulation; the resulting AM carrier was then filtered so that only a single sideband was transmitted (to minimise the bandwidth occupied by each call – see chapter 3). The exchange allocated different carrier frequencies to each call and then added all the transmissions together to form a complex signal and sent this into the trunk line.

The transmission system was essentially the same as that used for broadcasting radio and TV signals, where the available spectrum (i.e. the bandwidth of the trunk cable) is shared among the potential users. At the receiving exchange, the incoming mixture of frequencies was passed through an array of narrowband filters so as to recover and demodulate each call.

Time-division multiplexing on the telephone

Time-division multiplexing has been the main driving force in the globalisation of telephone communications. It has allowed a huge increase in signal traffic, both national and international, and reduced the costs to the user to such an extent that the telephone, in the developed world, has altered daily lifestyles. Witness the use of the mobile phone, the demise of the personal letter in favour of a telephone call or e-mail, the use of the Internet or working from a home linked by telephone line to an office.

TDM requires the information to be in digital form; the processing occurs at the telephone exchange (remember, the signal along the wire-pair from the home to the exchange is an analogue signal). The caller's voice is sampled 8000 times per second, in order to satisfy the Nyquist criterion (chapter 4). This sampling frequency has been chosen by international agreement: all the telecommunications

companies in the world use it. This means that, everywhere in the network, the time between one sample and the next is 125 μs.

SAQ 9.3

Show that the time between samples of a telephone call is 125 μs.

Each sample of a call is converted into a parallel binary word of eight bits and then further converted from parallel into serial. The exchange passes these eight bits into the trunk line as a digital signal, as shown in *figure 9.14a*. *Figure 9.14b* shows the digital signal on the line due to this one particular call; the bit duration is τ. It is important to distinguish between the time for one sample (8τ) and the time between the start of one sample and the start of the next (125 μs).

For the purpose of explanation, suppose the bit duration τ in a simple system is 3 μs (in real exchanges it is much shorter than this). Each sample will therefore last for 24 μs. This means that there is a dead time for each caller of 101 μs (i.e. 125 − 24 μs) when the caller does not need to be connected to the line. This 101 μs could be used to allow at least four other users access to the same line, because four other sets of samples, each of length 24 μs, can be fitted into 101 μs if very careful synchronisation is used.

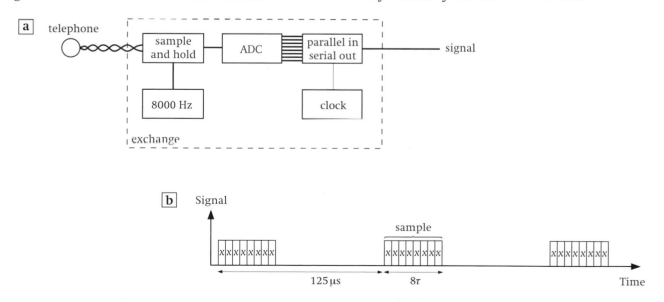

● **Figure 9.14** The digital signal produced by a single telephone call. In **a** the clock frequency $f = 1/\tau$, where τ is the bit duration. In **b** $x = 0$ or 1.

The synchronisation process can be imagined to be like a five-way rotating switch in each exchange. The five poles of the imaginary switch accommodate the five different pairs of users (i.e. the callers and their listeners) who are all to share the same line. The receiving exchange must arrange that the position of its 'switch' at any time corresponds to that of the 'switch' at the transmitting exchange. The switches would be synchronised to start in position 1 and stay there for 24 µs while the eight bits from a sample of call 1 are fed into and along the trunk line. Then the switches change to position 2 and stay there for 24 µs while the eight bits from a sample of call 2 are fed into the line. Then they change to position 3 for 24 µs, then to position 4 for 24 µs and finally to position 5 for 24 µs.

In the 5 µs left, the two exchanges resynchronise to start again in position 1, so that the next eight-bit sample from call 1 can be fed into the line, repeating the process. This means that the signal in the trunk line is a procession of 1s and 0s corresponding to the bits of one sample after another.

This simplified system of five users sharing a trunk line is shown in *figure 9.15* and it should be

remembered that in real exchanges there are no rotating switches (no moving parts). The electronic gating circuits *behave* as if there were such switches.

The system described above allowed five users to share the line, because the bit duration was taken to be 3 µs. This is unrealistically long: modern electronic circuits can operate so quickly that the bit duration is much shorter than 3 µs, as we now discuss.

The effect of bit duration on channel-carrying capacity

The time between voice samples in the telephone network is a constant 125 µs. If the bit duration in µs is τ then the time for which each sample needs to occupy the trunk line is 8τ. Therefore, the maximum number of callers that can share the line by TDM is given by $125/(8\tau)$.

If $\tau = 0.01$ µs (equivalent to half the period of a clock running at 50 MHz which is not really very fast in today's electronics) then 1562 callers could share the same line.

If $\tau = 0.001$ µs (equivalent to half the period of a clock running at 500 MHz, which is common in

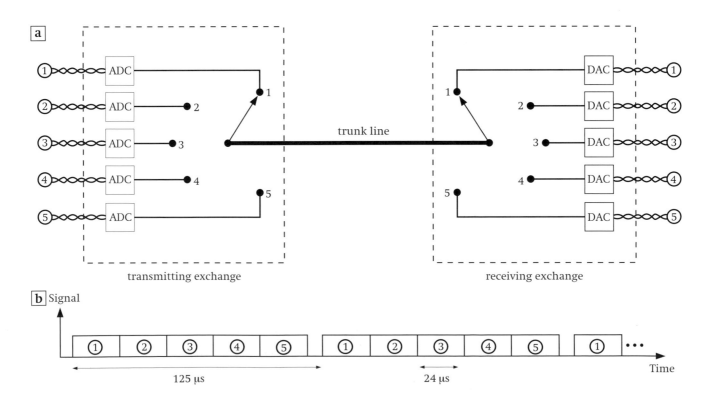

• **Figure 9.15** Time-division multiplexing (TDM) of five telephone calls. **a** Switching arrangement; **b** the signal stream.

today's electronics) then 15 625 callers could share the same line.

Our explanation of TDM has allowed no reserved time for control codes and assumed that the digital signals in the trunk line take no time to reach their destination exchange (which is clearly not so). These calculations are therefore somewhat simplistic. In a real TDM system, control and synchronisation codes have to be added to the stream of samples both to identify them and to keep the receiving exchange in step, so that all the samples maintain their correct relative positions (see chapter 4).

Time-division multiplexing in a modern exchange

The modern telephone system involves many layers of TDM, where streams of samples that are already time-division multiplexed are mixed with similar streams and multiplexed again, so that with each new division, the bit duration in the system gets shorter and shorter. This involves applying the signals to faster switches. *Figure 9.16* shows how a modern local exchange is set up to interleave calls by TDM. All the callers actively connected to the exchange (by wire-pairs) are organised into groups of 30. Each of these 30 calls is generating a digital signal at 64 kbit s^{-1} (i.e. 8000 × 8). Each group of 30 calls is multiplexed, together with two signalling channels (the control and synchronising data), to form a stream at 2 Mbit s^{-1} (i.e. 32 × 64 000). The 2 Mbit s^{-1} signal is carried by coaxial cable to an even higher-speed switch that accepts 63 of these cables and, by adding further control and synchronising codes, generates 155 Mbit s^{-1}. This is applied to an optic fibre, which is the trunk line. In this way, the digital signal in the optic fibre trunk line is carrying 63 × 30 = 1890 separate telephone calls.

When the 155 Mbit s^{-1} signal in the optic fibre is viewed as a function of time, it is seen to be composed of **frames**; each frame lasts for 125 μs. The frame starts with a synchronising header code H, which is followed by framing and control codes F and C; these are followed in turn by the 1890 eight-bit samples of 1890 separate phone calls. This is shown in *figure 9.17* overleaf.

Note again that all the telephone systems in the world have clocks that are locked to the same time interval, 125 μs. As a frame moves up

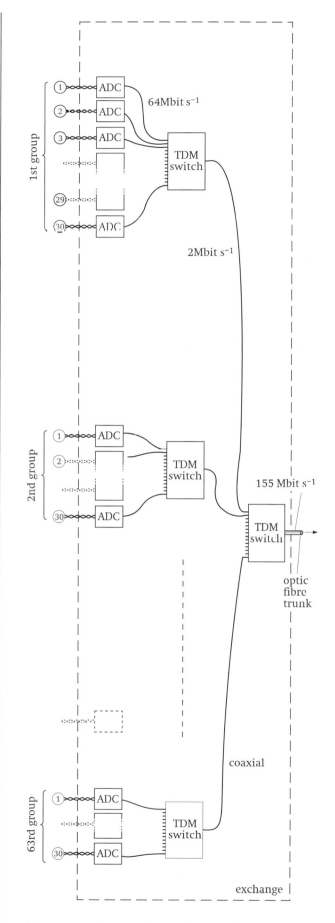

● **Figure 9.16** Layers of TDM in a modern exchange.

through higher exchanges, local to trunk to international, the clocks become more and more accurate. There are 16 levels of accuracy and each exchange essentially signals how accurate its clock is. Eventually, the system locks on to the best available clock. Moreover, further TDM occurs to **groups of frames** and there are now four different bit rates used in the national and international optic fibre trunk lines, as shown in *table 9.1*; at a bit rate of $10\,\text{Gbit s}^{-1}$, the optic-fibre trunk line can transmit about 10^5 phone calls. This means that about 2×10^5 users are sharing the same line, which results in a relatively low cost per user.

Optic-fibre bit rate (Mbit s^{-1})	Number of transmission channels
155	2016
622	8064
2500	32 256
10 000	129 024

● **Table 9.1** Bit rate and the corresponding number of channels. Most of the channels are occupied by phone call samples but some are reserved for signalling and control.

The mobile-phone system

In the 1970s, scientists from the Bell Laboratories in the United States put forward the idea of a mobile-phone network. It was not until the 1980s, however, that the idea became a working reality, first in the Nordic countries and then in the United States itself. In this system, the user carries a radio transmitter and receiver in a single handset. When operating, the handset establishes a radio-wave connection to a **base station** linked by a communications cable to a **cellular exchange**. The cellular exchange allows entry to the public switched telephone network (PSTN). This is shown in *figure 9.18*.

The range of carrier frequencies available to make the radio-wave connection is limited, yet the number of people who are likely to use the system is very large. It is thus essential to use the allocated radio spectrum as efficiently as possible, by **reusing** the same carrier frequencies, over and over again. This is done by:

■ using UHF frequencies, which have a limited terrestrial range; and

■ using low-power transmitters.

Early mobile-phone systems (i.e. until the 1990s) used analogue technology, with carrier frequencies in the range 917 to 960 MHz, modulated by narrow-band FM. The frequency deviation Δf_c of the carrier was 9.5 kHz and the voice frequency was limited to 3 kHz, so that the bandwidth occupied by each call was 25 kHz (see chapter 3). The base station transmitters used powers in the order of a few watts. Unfortunately, the use of analogue transmission made it relatively easy for an unauthorised person to tap phone calls using a scanner. Indeed, a number of famous people had their conversations recorded and sold to newspapers around the world. This is no longer possible, with modern digital systems.

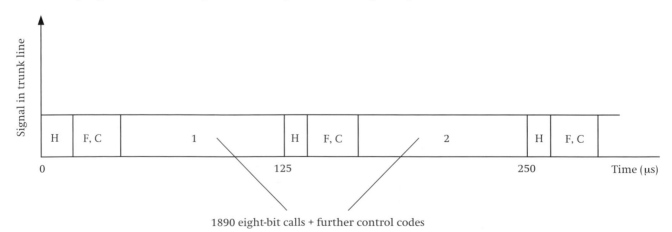

1890 eight-bit calls + further control codes

● **Figure 9.17** In a trunk line the information from 1890 calls is carried in frames, each of duration 125 µs. H, F and C refer to header, framing and control codes. '1' refers to the first set of eight-bit samples of 1890 separate phone calls, which includes further control codes, '2' refers to the second set and so on.

Communication link	Typical carrier frequency	Typical bandwidth of the information carried	Average distance between repeater amplifiers	Attenuation (at carrier frequency)
open wires on poles	baseband only	20 kHz	10 km	10 dB km^{-1}
wire-pairs	10 MHz	500 kHz	5 km	25 dB km^{-1}
coaxial cable	2 MHz (for telephone) 1 GHz (for cable TV)	1 MHz (for telephone) 400 MHz (for cable TV)	10 km (at 2 MHz) 100 m (at 1 GHz)	6 dB km^{-1} (at 2 MHz) 200 dB km^{-1} (at 1 GHz)
microwave links	5 GHz	100 MHz	40 km	depends on inverse square law
optic fibres	200 000 GHz	10 GHz	80 km	0.2 dB km^{-1}

● **Table 9.2** Summary of communication links and their characteristics.

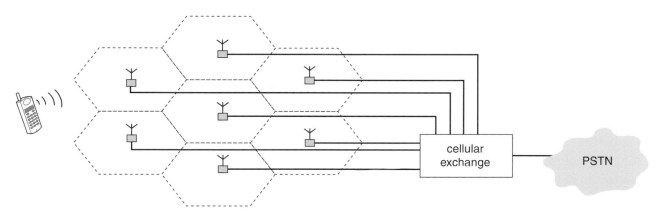

● **Figure 9.18** A group of base stations each linked by a cable to a cellular exchange and thence to the public switched telephone network.

In order to reuse the same carrier frequencies without interference, the country is divided into **cells**; in the middle of each cell there is a base station. Any handset operated in a particular cell will therefore communicate with that cell's base station. Each base station has an omnidirectional aerial, and the transmitted radio waves are powered so as to have a range approximately equal to the radius of the cell (usually a few kilometres). Neighbouring cells cannot use the same carrier frequencies, otherwise handsets used at the cell borders would experience interference. It is normal when drawing a **cellular radio** network (i.e. a mobile-phone network) to draw cells as hexagons because, unlike circles, hexagons tessellate, i.e. they fit together. A typical area of country covered by cells is shown in *figure 9.19*, where the numbers refer to the carrier frequencies allocated to the cell (i.e. cells with the same number use the same range

of carrier frequencies). In theory, this system can accommodate any number of users: either the cell size is decreased or smaller cells are added within larger ones.

When a handset is activated, it transmits an identifying signal, which will be picked up by a number of surrounding base stations. These base stations communicate the signal to the control computer at their cellular exchange. This computer then selects the base station with the strongest signal, usually the one closest to the handset, and allocates a channel (i.e. a carrier frequency) to that base station and handset. The cellular exchange monitors the handset signals and if they become too weak, e.g. if the handset is moving out of the cell, it will re-route the call through another base station.

The use of digital technology allows time-division multiplexing, which, in turn, allows the same carrier frequency to be shared by many different users. Each call is essentially allocated a particular time slot. In Europe, as in many other areas, a digital standard called GSM (global system

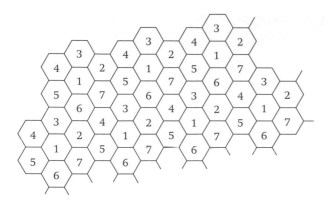

● **Figure 9.19** A cellular layout for a mobile-phone network.

for mobile communication) has been adopted so that, eventually, users will be able to make a call from any country using the system. Note that this system does not permanently allocate a particular frequency to a particular telephone. Instead, a particular range of frequencies is allocated to a particular cell. The base station selects a carrier frequency not in use at the time a handset makes contact and then tuning occurs to that frequency.

A simplified block diagram of the circuitry in the handset is shown in *figure 9.20*, where it may be seen that the microphone signal is amplified and converted to a digital signal. This signal is initially $64 \, \text{kbit s}^{-1}$ (i.e. 8000×8) but, by using digital compression and filtering circuits it can be reduced to $13 \, \text{kbit s}^{-1}$; this reduces speech quality slightly but saves on bandwidth. The compressed signal is then made to modulate an RF carrier

(selected from a range of frequencies of the order of a few GHz). The modulation technique is a variation on PSK (*figure 4.15*). The carriers in the allocated channel are spaced 200 kHz apart.

The signals to and from the handset are controlled by microprocessors. Two carrier frequencies are used: these are the **uplink** and the **downlink** frequencies (*figure 8.5*). These two carriers are kept 80 MHz apart. The transmission bit rate from each base station on any one particular carrier frequency is $270 \, \text{kbit s}^{-1}$ and this corresponds essentially to 20 time-division multiplexed calls.

SAQ 9.4
Suppose that carrier frequencies have to be spaced 200 kHz apart. Calculate the maximum number of downlink carrier frequencies which could be used from the range 1.85 GHz to 1.99 GHz.

There are four major companies in the UK providing independent mobile-phone systems, and this has resulted in about 10 000 cells and 40 000 base-station transmitting masts. These masts, with banks of aerials, can now be seen all over the country.

As more and more people purchase mobile phones, more and more masts will be required, because the cells will have to become smaller. If every person in the UK had a mobile phone then masts would have to be erected every few kilometres.

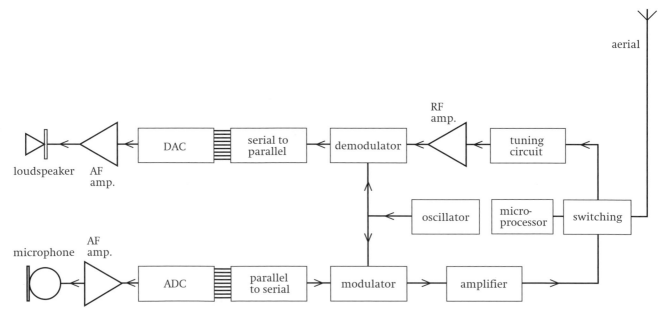

● **Figure 9.20** Simplified block diagram of a mobile-phone handset.

SUMMARY

◆ The telephone exchange was necessary because of the impracticality of connecting each pair of users by separate wires.

◆ Speaking into a telephone causes a modulated d.c. current in a pair of wires.

◆ Dual-tone multifrequency (DTMF) dialling is faster and more reliable than the original pulse dialling.

◆ Ringing involves sending voltage pulses through a capacitor and switch.

◆ Exchanges are linked by trunk lines; switching is now automated.

◆ Modern exchanges operate using time-slot switching.

◆ Telephone cables are wire-pair, coaxial cable or optic-fibre.

◆ A microwave link acts as a high-bandwidth wireless cable through the air.

◆ Originally, to maximise cable use and reduce costs FDM was used.

◆ Nowadays, the exchange digitises each call and uses TDM.

◆ Each phone call is composed of 8000 samples per second; each sample is eight bits long.

◆ TDM has resulted in a huge increase in traffic and a huge reduction in costs.

◆ The mobile-phone system relies on base stations in a cellular network; the same carrier frequencies are reused by non-neighbouring base stations.

◆ Mobile-phone systems are changing from analogue technology to digital technology.

Questions

1 Calculate the number of lines required for 10 users to be connected directly to each other (i.e. without an exchange).

2 Explain the fundamental difference between a user's line *to* a local exchange and a trunk line *from* that local exchange.

3 State and explain the advantages of coaxial cable over the original open-wire system for the transmission of telephone calls.

4 A particular telephone call between two users lasts for 25 minutes. Calculate the number of bits of information generated by this call. If each bit lasts for 0.02 μs, calculate the total length of time for which the two users actually used the line between them.

5 Suggest why it could be dangerous to the users of handsets if the cell radius in the mobile-phone system were chosen to be 50 km rather than 5 km.

CHAPTER 10

Optic fibres

By the end of this chapter you should be able to:

1 apply the laws of reflection and refraction to an optic fibre;

2 understand that there are several different types of optic fibre;

3 describe the propagation of light along *step-index fibres*;

4 understand the nature of the distortion produced by propagation down a step-index fibre and appreciate that this is reduced over long distances by using *mono-mode fibres*;

5 recall the types of light source and receiver used with optic fibres;

6 calculate *attenuation*, *signal power* and *noise power* in optic-fibre systems;

7 understand the uses of optic fibres for analogue signals and for digital signals.

Introduction

The physical phenomena of refraction and total internal reflection have been known and understood for over 150 years. Indeed, attempts were made over a century ago to guide light along a bent glass rod but they were not very successful, because the rod had to be supported somewhere and wherever it was clamped, light leaked out. This is shown in *figure 10.1*.

In the 1950s, Brian O'Brien developed the **clad fibre**, in which the glass rod was surrounded by an outer layer of glass, of lower refractive index, called **cladding**. It no longer mattered whether the cladding was touched because there was no light in it anyway; the light was confined to the **core**. This was the original **optic fibre** and is shown in *figure 10.2*.

In the 1950s, glass had a huge attenuation, of order $1000\,\mathrm{dB\,km^{-1}}$ (see chapter 5), so the original optic fibre was not thought usable for transmitting light more than a short distance. In 1966, however, Charles Kao and George Hockham published a paper in which they showed that the large attenuation in glass was due to the presence of impurities and was not a property of the glass itself. Thus optic fibre could be used for long-distance communication if the glass could be made pure enough. Following this suggestion, considerable research went into improving the purity of glass and by the 1970s, the attenuation had been so reduced that the telecommunications industry began to consider optic fibre as a serious alternative to coaxial cable. To appreciate just one of the many advantages of modern optic fibre over

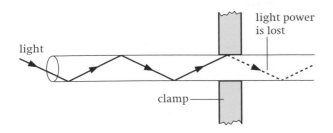

● **Figure 10.1** Light propagation in a solid glass rod.

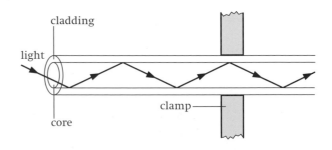

● **Figure 10.2** Light propagation in a clad fibre.

coaxial cable, compare the attenuation of the two types of cable, shown in *figure 10.3*; the horizontal scale is logarithmic.

In the 1980s, optic-fibre cable had developed so many advantages over coaxial cable that it caused a major upheaval in almost all cable communication systems. It was not only used for telephone lines, it was used for cable TV, office networks, computer links, remote monitoring equipment, transmitting signals in noisy environments, communicating signals in ships and aeroplanes; it can even be uncoiled, like a fishing line, from a moving missile so that a soldier can guide it onto a target he cannot directly see.

Refraction and total internal reflection

A measure of the optical density of a transparent medium or material is its refractive index (see *Physics 1* chapter 18). This is given the symbol n and defined by the following formula:

refractive index n of the material

$= \dfrac{\text{speed of light in a vacuum}}{\text{speed of light in the material}}$

Note that as there is no velocity greater than the velocity of light in a vacuum, there is no material with a refractive index less than unity.

When a light ray tries to pass from an optically less dense (smaller-n) medium into an optically more dense (larger-n) medium, it will always succeed. This is because the ray bends towards the normal (this is an imaginary line at right angles to the surface). *Figure 10.4a* shows a ray travelling from a vacuum into a transparent material. It can be shown from the definition above that

$$n = \frac{\sin i}{\sin r}$$

Figure 10.4b shows a ray travelling from material 1, with refractive index n_1, into material 2, with refractive index n_2. Our formula now becomes

$$n_1 \sin i_1 = n_2 \sin i_2 \quad \text{or} \quad \frac{n_2}{n_1} = \frac{\sin i_1}{\sin i_2}$$

Note that when medium 1 is a vacuum, so that $n_1 = 1$, we recover our original formula.

However, when a light ray tries to pass from an optically more dense into an optically less dense material then it may not succeed, because now

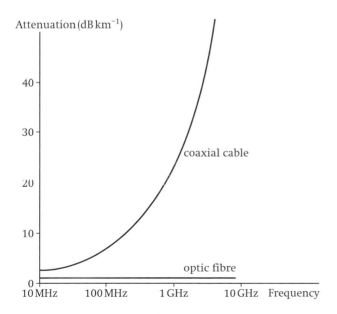

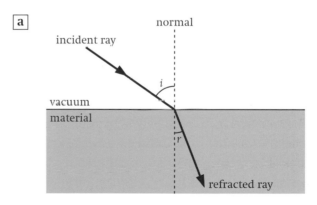

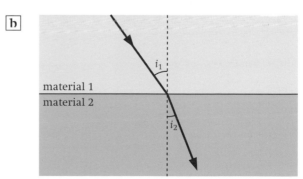

● **Figure 10.3** Attenuation in optic-fibre and coaxial cables. Note the logarithmic horizontal scale, i.e. each of the intervals corresponds to a factor-of-10 change in the frequency.

● **Figure 10.4** A light ray travelling **a** from a vacuum into a material and **b** from one material into another of higher refractive index.

the ray bends *away from* the normal.

If the angle of incidence is less than the **critical angle** i_c then the ray will pass through the boundary (*figure 10.5a*).

If the angle of incidence is equal to the critical angle, then the angle of refraction will be 90° (*figure 10.5b*).

If the angle of incidence is greater than the critical angle, then the refracted ray does not exist and all the energy of the incident ray is *reflected* at the boundary. This is known as **total internal reflection** and is shown in *figure 10.5c*.

Types of fibre

There are several different types of optic fibre, with different characteristics and uses. In **glass fibres**, the diameter of the core down which the light actually travels varies from below 10 μm up to 200 μm. The larger-diameter fibres are easier to splice (i.e. join together) and thus allow cheaper connectors to be used; they also allow much greater light power to flow through them but their ability to transmit high-frequency pulses is relatively poor and this considerably limits their use.

In **all-plastic fibres**, the core diameters can exceed 1 mm and this allows signals to be transmitted even when the fibre is poorly spliced or not well linked to the receiver. Many schools use these fibres to illustrate the principles of communication by total internal reflection. Such fibres, however, have a relatively high attenuation (of order 150 dB km^{-1}) and limited transmission bandwidth, so they are not normally used in the telecommunications industry. They are most

efficient with visible light (especially red light of about 650 nm); an example of their use is in certain types of motor car, where they form a link between a headlamp and the dashboard; if the fibre glows, the driver knows the headlamp is working.

Step-index multimode glass fibre

As mentioned earlier, the cladding of a glass fibre has a lower refractive index than that of the core. This is described as **step-index** construction (*figure 10.6*). The core in a step-index multimode glass fibre (see below) is usually about 100 μm in diameter and the cladding is about 20 μm thick. The fibre is composed of a very pure and uniform glass core, surrounded by a very pure and uniform glass cladding. The refractive index of the core must be greater than the refractive index of the cladding (otherwise the fibre will not work). A ray of light launched into the core at an angle of incidence greater than the critical angle between the core–cladding boundary, will suffer total internal reflection in the core. This ray will therefore not be able to escape from the core but will travel along until it emerges at the other end of the fibre. Note that the difference in refractive index n between the core and the cladding is only about 1%. Typical values of n are 1.500 for the core and 1.485 for the cladding.

SAQ 10.1

The refractive index of the core in an optic fibre is 1.500 and that of the cladding is 1.485. Calculate the critical angle i_c at the boundary between them.

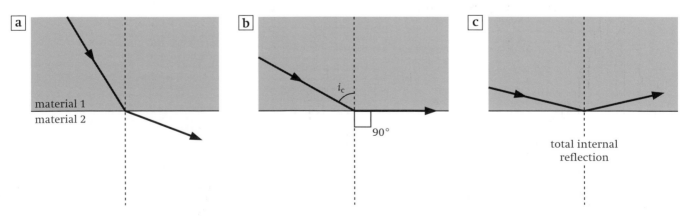

- **Figure 10.5** A light ray travelling in one material is incident at an interface with a material of lower refractive index **a** at an angle less than the critical angle i_c, **b** at i_c, **c** at an angle greater than i_c.

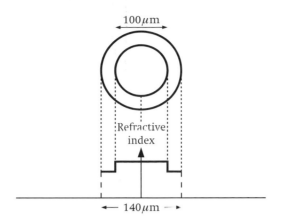

- **Figure 10.6** A step-index multimode fibre.

The meaning of multimode

The light that propagates down the core of a **multimode fibre** is composed of various **modes**. At a simple level, a mode can be treated as a group of light rays that enter the fibre at the same angle. This is shown in *figure 10.7*. A light ray that makes few reflections in travelling down the core is called a *low-order mode* while one that makes many reflections is called a *high-order mode*. The number of different modes that can propagate in a fibre is a function of the core diameter and the wavelength of the light.

Dispersion

Imagine launching a brief light pulse into a multimode fibre. This can be done by switching on a light-emitting diode (LED) at the entrance to the core and switching it off a few microseconds later. This light pulse will be composed of rays that are not all of the same wavelength or going in the same direction. This causes two fundamental problems, **material dispersion** and **modal dispersion**, the combined effects of which are shown in *figure 10.8*.

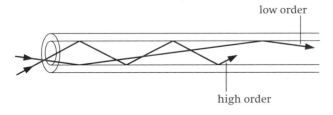

- **Figure 10.7** Propagation modes in a step-index multimode fibre.

■ **Material dispersion**

The refractive index of glass is not a fixed constant but varies with the wavelength of the light (witness the creation of a spectrum of white light by a glass prism). If a pulse is composed of rays of light of different wavelengths then, even if they travel the same path, different rays will take different times to get to the end of the fibre. This effect causes the output pulse to stretch in time.

■ **Modal (or multipath) dispersion**

Even if all the rays of light were of the same wavelength, they would not strike the interface at the same angle. Therefore they would not propagate along the fibre in the same mode. In other words, they do not follow the same path; the lowest-order mode, travelling straight down the core, reaches the end before the highest-order mode, which makes the most reflections down the core. This effect also causes the output pulse to stretch in time.

If a progression of high-frequency pulses is applied to a long multimode fibre then by the time the pulses reach the other end of the fibre they will have merged together by dispersion and be unresolvable. This is known as **smearing** and is shown in *figure 10.9*.

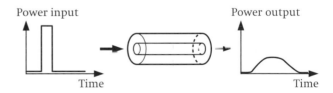

- **Figure 10.8** The effects of dispersion on an output pulse.

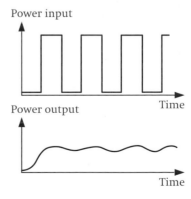

- **Figure 10.9** Smearing of a pulse in a step-index multimode fibre.

Dispersion puts severe restrictions on the use of multimode fibres and they are only used for high bit rates over very short distances (or low bit rates over longer distances). Normally they would not be used for any distance greater than about 1 km.

SAQ 10.2

A step-index multimode fibre has length 6 km and core diameter 100 μm. The refractive index of the core is 1.5 and the critical angle at the core–cladding boundary is 82°. Calculate the time taken for a light ray to travel **a** directly down the central core axis, **b** by the greatest number of reflections.

Graded-index multimode glass fibre

In graded-index fibres the refractive index of the core changes gradually to meet that of the cladding (*figure 10.10*). **Graded-index** multimode fibres have smaller-diameter cores than step-index multimode fibres, typically about 65 μm rather than 100 μm. The centre of the core is where the refractive index reaches a maximum; the core is produced by heating about two hundred layers of glass, with gradually changing composition, and then drawing the composite material into a fibre.

The gradient in the refractive index gradually bends all non-axial rays back towards the axis. The refractive index curve in *figure 10.10* is a parabola, and it can be shown that this causes the rays to follow a **sine-wave path** down the fibre. Light rays from the same pulse entering the fibre at different angles will follow sine-wave paths of different amplitude and thus take routes of different length down the core. However, rays on the sine-wave path with the largest amplitude have spent more time in the outer parts of the core where the light speed is greatest (remember, the lower the refractive index the faster the light speed). The two effects compensate, and so the net result is that if a number of rays are launched into the fibre at the same time then they reach the end of the fibre nearly together, regardless of the actual path each has followed down the fibre. Two paths are shown in *figure 10.11*.

Graded-index fibres therefore give a considerable reduction in modal (multipath) dispersion, so this type of fibre can carry higher frequency pulses for a

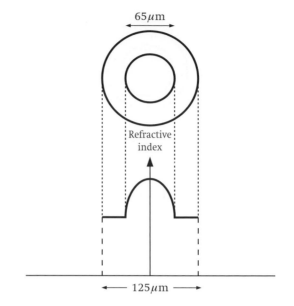

● **Figure 10.10** A graded-index fibre. The refractive index of the core is a parabolic function of distance; its maximum value is about 2% greater than that of the cladding.

greater distance than step-index multimode fibres. They allow the use of (cheap) LEDs, rather than (expensive) semi-conductor lasers and they also allow connectors with looser tolerances. However, graded-index fibres are not used for any long-distance transmissions in the telecommunications industry; they find a limited use in short data links or local area networks (see chapter 11). The most important and widely used fibre is monomode fibre, which we now discuss.

Step-index monomode glass fibre

The core in **monomode** fibres is usually about 9 μm in diameter and the cladding is 125 μm in diameter. The core is arranged to be about seven times the wavelength of the light which is to pass down it. In this low-diameter core the electromagnetic wave will propagate in a single mode and all modal (multipath) dispersion is eliminated. Such a fibre is shown in *figure 10.12*. Conventional ray optics cannot properly describe the behaviour of light in a monomode fibre because the fibre is essentially behaving as a wave guide. It is something of an over-simplification to say that light can only travel directly down the fibre. Step-index monomode fibres are now used by telecommunications companies all over the world for the long-distance transmission of both analogue and digital signals.

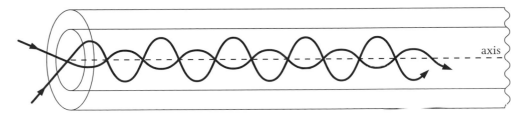

● **Figure 10.11** Propagation of light rays in a graded-index fibre: each ray propagates in a sine wave.

Attenuation, light sources and receivers

Attenuation

When the attenuation (i.e. the power loss in dB km^{-1}) for the core glass in an optic fibre is plotted as a function of the wavelength, the result is the graph shown in *figure 10.13*. Clearly, the most appropriate wavelengths to use are those that give the lowest attenuation; the graph reveals a minimum attenuation at two infrared frequencies, 1310 nm and 1550 nm, 1550 nm having the lower attenuation. However, until recently the 1310 nm wavelength was the one most commonly used because the laser that emitted 1550 nm light could not be directly modulated.

Light sources

Optic-fibre systems make use of two types of semiconductor light source: light emitting diodes and semiconductor lasers (sometimes called diode lasers). Outputs from these two types of source are shown in *figure 10.14*. Which source is used depends on the particular application: LEDs are used for relatively low frequencies over relatively short distances and lasers are used for high frequency transmission over long distances.

Overall, the laser is by far the superior light source, for two reasons.

■ Because of its narrow beam, a much higher light power can be injected into the fibre, so that the uninterrupted transmission distance (before amplification or regeneration becomes necessary) is greater;

■ the laser emits a very narrow range of wavelengths, so the effect of material dispersion on pulse width is almost negligible.

Note, however, that the LED is cheaper and has a longer lifetime than a laser.

SAQ 10.3

Suggest why the LED is not used as a light source for monomode fibres.

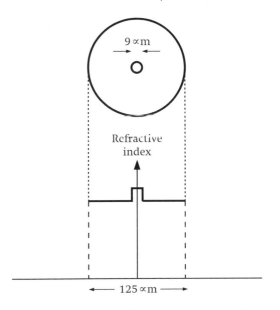

● **Figure 10.12** A step-index monomode fibre.

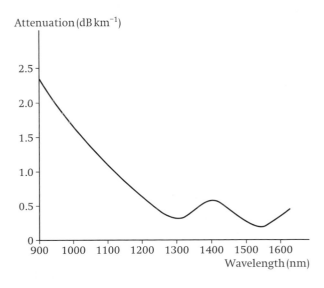

● **Figure 10.13** Attenuation in the core of a monomode fibre.

Light receivers

The detectors used in optic-fibre systems are almost always photodiodes (although phototransistors are sometimes used). These devices are connected in reverse bias so that in the dark they prevent current flow; there is almost no leakage current. When light of the appropriate wavelength falls on them, a small current flows; it is roughly proportional to the received light intensity. A typical detector circuit is shown in *figure 10.15*.

The wavelength response of photodiodes depends on their composition; they can be made from silicon, germanium, gallium arsenide, indium phosphide or some compound of these. Silicon detectors are insensitive to wavelengths longer than 1000 nm, so the 1310 nm photodiode is manufactured from indium gallium arsenide. The sensitivity of this detector is about 0.6 µA per µW.

Launch power and noise in a monomode optic-fibre system

For the transmission of analogue or digital signals into a monomode fibre, the infrared laser must inject, or **launch**, a relatively powerful light beam into the tiny-diameter core. Typical launch powers range from about 40 mW, for high-power long-distance transmission, to a few mW for shorter distances.

The maximum uninterrupted transmission distance is governed by the need to keep the signal-to-noise ratio above a certain minimum value (see chapter 5). This will vary with the nature of the transmission: for example, analogue cable TV signals must maintain a high signal-to-noise ratio while in digitised telephone signals the signal-to-noise ratio can be slightly lower. The maximum distance also depends upon the wavelengths used (i.e. around 1300 nm or 1550 nm; see the discussion above on attenuation). The points to bear in mind for this process are outlined below.

- Once the light signal has been launched into the fibre it will carry some of the inherent electrical noise of the transmitter. This slightly contaminated light will travel down the fibre and gradually lose energy as it does so.
- The noise contribution from the fibre itself is virtually zero.
- When the light reaches the receiver it will cause a current in the photodiode.
- The photodiode, however, will always produce some current, even in the dark. This is known as the **dark current** of the receiver. The dark current sets a limit to the minimum detectable light signal.

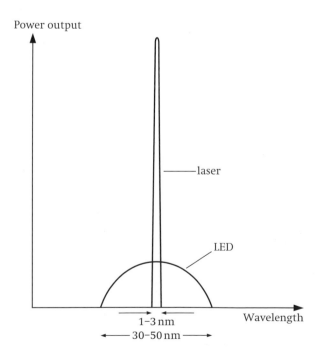

● **Figure 10.14** Outputs of a laser and of a light-emitting diode (LED).

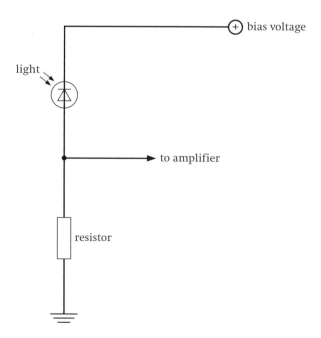

● **Figure 10.15** A photodiode detector circuit.

Thus the noise level in the system is mainly set by the dark current in the receiving photodiode, and this will depend on the type of photodiode being used, the operating temperature and the bias voltage. Normally, this noise power is of the order of microwatts.

When a brief pulse, caused by switching on and off a laser or LED, enters a length of optic fibre the power input as a function of time will be more or less rectangular in shape. The pulse output from the receiver, however, will be the randomly outlined hump shown in *figure 10.16*. The received pulse has this shape for three reasons.

■ The area under the power–time graph, which represents the energy in the pulse, is smaller because of attenuation in the fibre.
■ The duration of the pulse is longer, because of dispersion in the fibre.
■ The randomly changing outline represents noise picked up in the receiver.

Amplifying light signals in optic fibres

When a long optic-fibre cable, such as a telephone trunk line, a cable TV line or an Internet link, has to be broken up into sections because of attenuation, then at each junction the light signal has to be amplified. There are two ways in which this can be done, by electrical or optical amplification, as shown in *figure 10.17*.

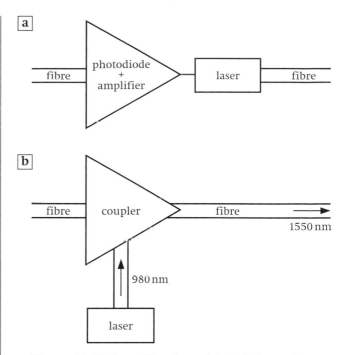

● **Figure 10.17** Amplification of signals in optic fibres can be either **a** electrical or **b** optical.

■ **Electrical amplification**
In this method, the arriving light signal is detected by a photodiode and converted into an electrical signal. The electrical signal is then amplified by an electronic amplifier. The amplifier output drives and modulates a laser, which recreates the original light signal. Most optic-fibre systems at the present time use this method, because they use a 1310 nm carrier and optical amplifiers work best at 1550 nm.

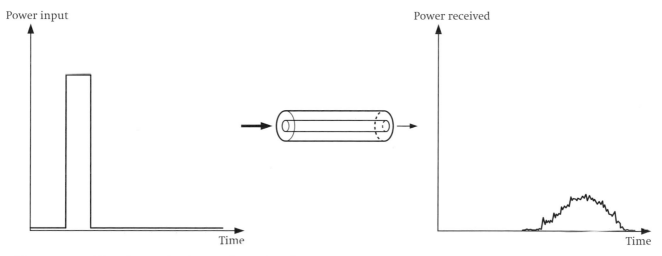

● **Figure 10.16** The change in shape of a pulse after transmission through an optic fibre.

■ **Optical amplification**

In this method, the arriving 1550 nm light signal enters an **optocoupler** (a device coupling two light systems),which is also fed by a 980 nm laser. For each 1550 nm signal photon that passes through the coupler another 1550 nm photon is released from the energy field created by the 980 nm laser. This works on the same stimulated emission principle that governs the operation of a laser.

It is expected that, in the future, most amplification will be done optically rather than electrically: optical amplifiers have very low noise levels and can easily amplify signals of widely varying bit rates. They are also able to amplify signals at slightly different wavelengths within their operating range (e.g. 1530–1550 nm) without interference between these wavelengths. This will allow cable companies to increase their transmission capacity.

Wavelength-division multiplexing in optic fibres

Nowadays, there is increasing use of several light carrier waves in the same fibre core. Each carrier wave has a different wavelength and is independently modulated. The various modulated light signals propagate down the fibre without interfering and at the receiver they are separated optically before being processed. In this way, a cable company can significantly increase its carrying capacity without having to lay any more cables. This process is called **wavelength-division multiplexing** and at the present time, 20 different carrier wavelengths can be squeezed down a single fibre.

Cable television

There is an extensive network in many countries of optic-fibre cable-carrying TV signals. Although it is expected that during the next five to ten years all TV signals will become digital (both in broadcasting and in cable), at the present time there is still a widely used analogue communication system for TV signals in optic fibres. For example, in the UK, there is an analogue system that operates as follows.

1 Each TV channel is composed of four modulated carriers, V, C, FM and N. V is the video (brightness), C is the colour, FM is the sound and N is nicam stereo.

2 The information on these four carriers must fit into a baseband of under 8 MHz, because this is the frequency range by which each TV channel in the allocated spectrum is separated.

3 The cable TV company may use carriers in the frequency range 72–522 MHz although some of this spectrum is prohibited to them. For example, 88–108 MHz is used for broadcast FM radio; 108–118 MHz is used for airport location beacons; 472–862 MHz is used for terrestrial TV broadcasts.

4 The cable TV company can frequency-division-multiplex up to 52 separate TV channels, and this effectively involves allocating 4 × 52 = 208 different carrier frequencies from the available spectrum.

5 The 208 modulated carriers are then added together to form a highly complex analogue signal, which is made to modulate the light intensity of a 1310 nm laser feeding a monomode fibre.

6 At the receiving end of the fibre, after the light signal has been reconverted to an electrical one, 52 filter circuits (each with a pass band of 8 MHz) separate out the individual TV channels.

The advantages of optic fibre over coaxial cable

The reasons for the change to optic fibre from coaxial cable are summarised below.

■ Glass is an extremely common substance and is cheaper than copper.

■ The cables are much thinner and lighter.

■ They have a much lower attenuation and so allow much greater distances of uninterrupted transmission.

■ Optic fibre has a much higher bandwidth and therefore a much greater information-carrying capacity.

■ Optic fibres are immune to electromagnetic interference and so can be used in noisy environments.

■ They do not radiate energy, so there is no crosstalk between adjacent fibres.

- They are very secure, because they cannot be tapped.
- They are ideal channels for digital signals in the form of light pulses.

Worked example

The telecommunications industry uses 1 mW as a reference signal power; signal powers that are measured against it are said to be in dBm.

A signal power of 16 dBm is input to an optic fibre. The optic fibre has an attenuation of $0.20\,\text{dB km}^{-1}$. The signal is transmitted for 50 km uninterrupted. The received signal-to-noise ratio is 40 dB. Calculate **a** the light power P_L launched into the fibre; **b** the light power P_R reaching the receiver; **c** the effective noise level P_N in the receiver circuit.

Solution:

a The power launched is given by
$$16 = 10\lg\,(P_L/1\,\text{mW})$$
Thus
$$P_L = 10^{1.6} \times 1\,\text{mW}$$
$$= 40\,\text{mW}$$

b The total attenuation $= 50 \times (-0.20)$
$$= -10\,\text{dB}$$
$$= 10\lg\,(P_R/40\,\text{mW})$$
Thus
$$P_R = 10^{-1} \times 40\,\text{mW}$$
$$= 4\,\text{mW}$$

c If the signal-to-noise ratio is 40 dB then
$$40 = 10\lg\,(4/P_N)$$
$$10^4 = 4/P_N$$
$$P_N = 0.4\,\mu\text{W}$$

Optic fibre data

Analogue signals in optic fibre (cable TV)

The maximum launch power of signal into fibre is 40 mW.
The signal-to-noise ratio is kept above 40 dB.
With a 1310 nm laser, the maximum repeater spacing is 30 km.
With a 1550 nm laser, the maximum repeater spacing is 50 km.

Digital signals in optic fibre (telephone or Internet)

The maximum launch power of the signal into the fibre is about 10 mW.
The signal-to-noise ratio is kept above 30 dB.
With a 1310 nm laser, the maximum repeater spacing is 60 km.
With a 1550 nm laser, the maximum repeater spacing is 90 km.
The maximum bit rate is in excess of $10\,\text{Gbit s}^{-1}$.

Note that uninterrupted distances in excess of 160 km have been obtained with light signals in optic fibres.

SUMMARY

- Optic fibres are composed of a central core surrounded by a cladding.

- Pure glass has a very low attenuation or power loss.

- The refractive index of the core must be greater than that of the cladding.

- Plastic fibres operate with visible light and have few uses in telecommunications.

- Step-index multimode fibres are only useful for low bit rates over short distances.

- Multimode fibres suffer from material and modal dispersion.

- Graded-index fibres minimise modal dispersion but are not widely used owing to cost.

- Monomode fibres do not suffer from modal dispersion; they use infrared lasers to minimise material dispersion. Thus they allow large distances of uninterrupted transmission.

- Light sources can be LEDs or lasers; light receivers are photodiodes.

- The noise level is effectively set by the dark current of the photodiode.

- Optic-fibre signals may be amplified electrically or optically.

- Wavelength-division multiplexing is used to increase the carrying capacity of an optic fibre.

Questions

1   A monomode optic-fibre telephone cable links London and New York. The cable has a total length of 6000 km and the core has a refractive index of 1.5. Calculate the conversation time-delay resulting from light travel through the core of the fibre.

2   A 2 mW light signal enters an optic fibre with an attenuation of 0.3 dB km^{-1}. If the fibre is 15 km long, calculate the light power received by the other end.

3   A light signal of input power 30 mW is applied to an optic fibre with an attenuation of 0.2 dB km^{-1}. The fibre is 35 km in length. At the receiver, the signal-to-noise ratio is 28 dB. Calculate the light power reaching the receiver and the effective noise power in the receiver.

4   In an electric train there are d.c. motors and extensive electrical machinery. Explain why cables from various sensors to the driver's dashboard would be better made from optic fibre than copper cable.

CHAPTER 11

The Internet

By the end of this chapter you should be able to:

1 understand the advantages and disadvantages of different types of network;

2 understand the origins of the *Internet*;

3 outline how information is transferred using the Internet, including the *World Wide Web*, *file transfer protocol* and *e-mail*;

4 understand the use of the Internet for multimedia communications;

5 demonstrate an awareness of social, economic, environmental and technological changes arising from modern communication methods, including the advent of tele-working from home.

Networks

All over the world there are many networks, usually set up to link either telephones or computers. The network may be an isolated **local area network** (LAN) within a building or it could be a **metropolitan area network** (MAN) linking businesses and institutions within a city. The public switched telephone network (PSTN) is an example of a collection of national **wide area networks** (WANs) that have been interlinked to form the most extensive man-made structure on Earth.

A **network** is a set of **links** by which a number of users (i.e. transmitters and receivers of information) are interconnected. The links are made between **nodes**, which are **switching points** where the information is made to pass in a particular direction. The way in which the users are connected in a network is known as the **topology** of the network; three topologies for five users are described below.

Mesh network

In a mesh network, each user is connected to a node and every node is connected to every other node. This is shown in *figure 11.1*, where it should be noted that a large number of transmission

routes are possible between any two users. To understand the operation, imagine that user 2 at node 2 is to send a message to user 4 at node 4. The routes by which this information could travel from 2 to 4 are as follows:

$2 \rightarrow 4$

$2 \rightarrow 1 \rightarrow 4$

$2 \rightarrow 3 \rightarrow 4$

$2 \rightarrow 5 \rightarrow 4$

$2 \rightarrow 1 \rightarrow 5 \rightarrow 4$

$2 \rightarrow 1 \rightarrow 3 \rightarrow 4$

$2 \rightarrow 1 \rightarrow 5 \rightarrow 3 \rightarrow 4$

$2 \rightarrow 1 \rightarrow 3 \rightarrow 5 \rightarrow 4$

$2 \rightarrow 3 \rightarrow 1 \rightarrow 4$

$2 \rightarrow 3 \rightarrow 5 \rightarrow 4$

$2 \rightarrow 3 \rightarrow 1 \rightarrow 5 \rightarrow 4$

This system has the advantage that if a link is broken, if a node fails or if there is traffic congestion at a particular node then the communication can be re-routed and hence still made. Unfortunately, a fully interconnected mesh network would be very expensive to instal and operate and thus it is often the case that several links are omitted. Nevertheless, this system is sometimes used for wide area networks.

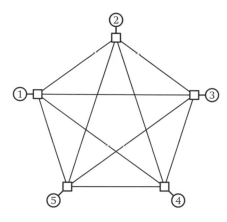

● **Figure 11.1** A mesh network. The users are represented by numbered circles and the nodes by small squares. The nodes are all connected by communication links.

Star network

In a star network, the users are all connected to a single node as shown in *figure 11.2*. In this system, there is only one possible route by which any user may send a message to any other user and if the node fails then the entire network is shut down. This system is used for local calls to and from local telephone exchanges. It is also sometimes used for a local area network that serves the needs of a single building or small complex of buildings.

Ring network

In a ring network, each node is connected to its two nearest nodes; the links form a ring. There are thus two routes by which any two users may communicate, so if a link is broken or a node fails then the message can still be transmitted in the opposite direction. This system can be used for local area networks as well as major backbones such as the interconnections between telephone

exchanges. This is shown in *figure 11.3*. A **backbone** is a high-capacity, high-speed dedicated line. Modern backbones can transfer data at a rate of 2.4 Gbit s^{-1}.

SAQ 11.1

Four users are located at each of the corners of a square of length 100 m. A network is to be set up such that a communication pathway exists between any two users. Calculate the minimum length of cable required to set up **a** a mesh network, **b** a star network, **c** a ring network.

Data

If the information which is to be communicated through a network is derived from a computer memory, then it will be in binary-coded form and as such is referred to as **data**. When the data is transferred, or switched, through nodes, then it requires the use of several computers for all the processes involved in the transfer, such as decision making and control, timing, encoding and decoding, error detection and storage.

A brief history of the Internet

In 1958, the United States Advanced Research Projects Agency (ARPA) had the idea of linking a small number of computers together so that their various programming facilities could be shared by their users. The motivation was that the computers of the time were very large and hugely expensive and the types of problem addressed on one machine were not necessarily the same as those on

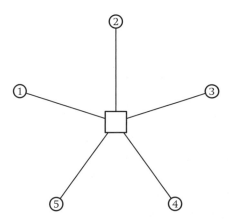

● **Figure 11.2** A star network.

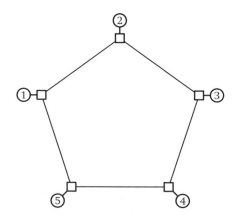

● **Figure 11.3** A ring network.

another. The resulting computer network was called the ARPANET and it was only used by experts. As this network expanded, however, it began to experience problems in transferring the ever increasing volume of information, or data, which was being generated. By the 1960s, the controllers of the network had solved this problem by breaking up the information to be transmitted into packets that could be intelligently routed to the destination computer. This process was known as **packet switching** (see below).

By the 1970s, the ARPANET had grown further to include the computers situated in a large number of universities and scientific establishments. These computers, however, usually had different operating systems running different programming languages. It was essential, therefore, that before any machine could be connected to the network it was programmed to obey a common set of rules for the transmission and reception of data. These rules became known as **protocols** (see below).

There were two main uses of the ARPANET at this time; one was **Telnet**, which enabled scientists to run their programs on more powerful computers located elsewhere, and the other was **e-mail** (i.e. electronic mail). E-mail allowed scientists an efficient and easy means of communication and this soon meant that e-mail dominated the use of the network.

Also in the 1970s, a user-friendly operating system called UNIX (which was created by Bell Telephone Laboratories) allowed enthusiasts to write software and build simple modems that enabled their computers to link up through the telephone network. Thus, anyone with the appropriate equipment could access the databases and facilities of the ARPANET through their telephone lines. As a result, a user's information-exchange network, called USENET, was established in which groups of like-minded people linked up to discuss specialist topics of interest.

By the early 1980s, USENET groups and individuals, in both America and Europe, were making so much independent use of the ARPANET that the operators eventually relinquished control and allowed the system to become what is now known as the **Internet**. The Internet is thus an *inter*connection of *networks*, which are nowadays linked together by backbones.

Many universities, private companies and government agencies fund and run their own networks (which could be a local area network or an **intranet**), which are now connected to the backbones of the Internet. The backbones themselves are funded and run by different government and private organisations. The Internet as a whole is owned and controlled by no individual body or organisation.

How the Internet works

The Internet allows one user's computer system (called the **client**) to send a coded digital signal to another user's computer system (called the **server**), requesting that it send the client information from the server's database or memory. The processes of requesting and receiving this information are governed by a number of rules or **protocols**, which have been established by international agreement.

In the late 1980s, the International Standards Organisation (which sets standards for business machines and computers) invented a framework, or architecture, by which two computers, separated by some distance, should communicate. This framework is called the **open systems interconnection** (OSI) and it enables different makes of computer with different operating systems to exchange data, either through dedicated lines or through telephone lines. To conform to the OSI model, each computer system is made up of seven layers. Data to be transferred originates in layer 7 of the transmitting computer system and goes down through various other layers (each of which performs a function) until, prepared for transmission, it reaches layer 1. Data received arrives at layer 1 and then proceeds up through its various layers until it arrives at the destination layer, 7. This is shown in *figure 11.4*.

At the transmitting end, as the data moves down from one layer to the next each layer adds its own header, so that the digital signal grows longer and longer. At the receiving end, each header is removed by the corresponding layer until the original data reaches layer 7. The functions of the seven layers are shown in *table 11.1*.

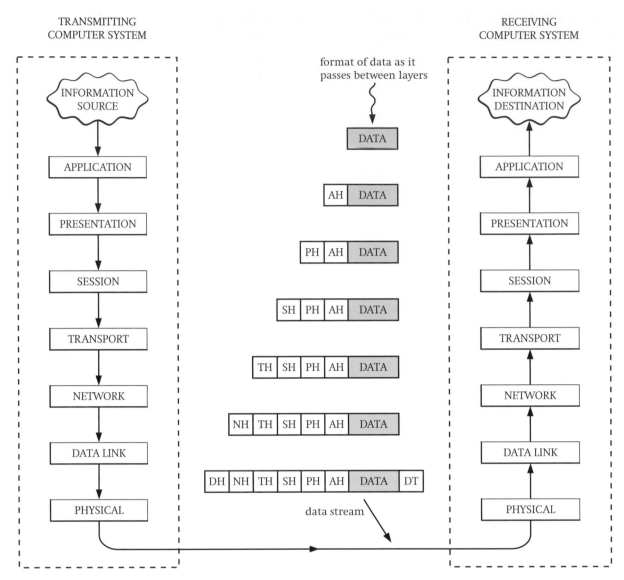

TRANSMITTING COMPUTER SYSTEM

RECEIVING COMPUTER SYSTEM

format of data as it passes between layers

- **Figure 11.4** Open systems interconnection (OSI) framework for computer-to-computer communication. The format abbreviations are explained in *table 11.1*.

Protocols

A protocol is a set of rules or procedures governing particular applications or processes. As long as users agree on the protocols then they are able to communicate. There are many protocols used in the various applications carried out on the Internet. Some of these are as follows.

■ **Serial-line Internet protocol** (SLIP)
This allows a computer to be connected to the Internet through a modem. It is a software routine used when dialling into an Internet service provider (ISP).

■ **Point-to-point protocol** (PPP)
This is a more modern version of SLIP, which allows garbled packets to be retransmitted and thus is more error-free.

■ **File transfer protocol** (FTP)
This governs the transfer of a **file**, i.e. a block of data, from one computer (the server) to another computer (the client).

■ **Hypertext transfer protocol** (HTTP)
This governs the downloading of files from the World Wide Web (but is not as efficient as FTP).

■ **Transmission control protocol** (TCP)
This breaks down information to be communicated into packets (see below) before transmission and reassembles the packets on arrival.

■ **Internet protocol** (IP)
This ensures that packets are sent to the correct

Layer	Action when transmitting	Action when receiving
application	organises information from source, adds application header (AH)	removes AH, passes data to receiver
presentation	translates user data to receiver code, performs encryption, adds presentation header (PH)	removes PH, deciphers and converts to receiver code
session	defines beginning and end of applications message, provides checks against failure, adds session header (SH)	removes SH, holds until all data is received
transport	may break data into segments, adds transport header (TH)	removes TH, if data was broken up, waits for all parts to arrive and reassembles
network	adds sequence numbers to broken-up data, adds destination address of data packets, adds network header (NH)	removes NH, verifies destination address and sequence number, waits for all packets to arrive and reassembles
data link	adds data link header (DH) and data link trailer (DT) to form a TDM frame	removes DH and DT, checks whether any errors occurred in frame transfer
physical	transmits each frame as a sequence of bits	receives each frame and reconstructs data stream

● Table 11.1

destination. Each IP address on the Internet is composed of four numbers separated by dots (e.g. 143.57.184.92).

To see how protocols are used, suppose you wish to send an e-mail to a friend from your computer, which is pre-programmed (with PPP) to allow Internet access. The message you have typed becomes the data at the top of the seven layers of the OSI framework outlined in *table 11.1*. The e-mail application produces the protocol specification (i.e. the procedures that have to be employed to transfer your data) shown in *table 11.2*. As your message, i.e. your data, is processed through the various software layers of your computer it grows longer and longer, as shown in the central column in *figure 11.4*.

This particular application of the Internet (i.e. e-mail) is effectively governed by the header codes that are added to the data as the data progresses down the layers of the OSI transmission system in your computer. The applications protocol is effectively subsumed into the transmission control protocol (TCP), then into the Internet protocol (IP) and then into the ethernet protocol. The digital

Application	e-mail
presentation	simple mail transfer protocol (SMTP)
session	transmission control protocol (TCP)
transport	internet protocol (IP)
network	ethernet protocol (Allows data transfer at up to 100 Mbits s^{-1})
data link	data link
physical	this is the network from you to your friend

● Table 11.2 E-mail protocols.

signal representing your data as a function of time (called a **datagram**), as it passes through the network layer (i.e. after the ethernet protocol has been added), is shown in *figure 11.5*. The header of your datagram, at this point, is composed of 14 blocks, and each block is composed of a group of bits of code. The meaning, length and action of these codes are given in *table 11.3*.

File transfer and packet switching

Suppose a client has sent a request to a server to transmit a file (or document) made up of a large amount of data. If the server tried to transmit the

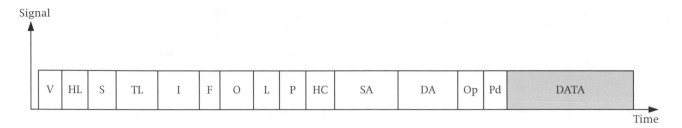

● **Figure 11.5** An Internet protocol datagram.

Code	Meaning	Action
V	version (4 bits)	identifies version of IP in use
HL	header length (4 bits)	specifies length of IP header
S	service (8 bits)	specifies desired reliability and throughput
TL	total length (16 bits)	identifies length of datagram (max. length 65 536 bits)
I	identification (16 bits)	sequence number
F	flag (3 bits)	permits or prohibits fragmentation of datagram
O	offset (13 bits)	if fragmentation is allowed this indicates where it belongs
L	time to live (8 bits)	measured in gateway transfers
P	protocol (8 bits)	identifies the next level of protocol to receive data
HC	header checksum (16 bits)	performs error check on header
SA	source address (32 bits)	the address of the transmitter
DA	destination address (32 bits)	the address of the receiver
Op	options (variable no. bits)	requests specific routing, handling and other services
Pd	padding (variable no. bits)	ensures header length is a multiple of four octets

● **Table 11.3** Each protocol has two forms of operation, one for client computers requesting a service and the other for server computers providing the service.

entire block of data in one transmission, the Internet protocol (IP) could not handle it. However, the data must pass through the layer containing the transmission control protocol (TCP) before it meets the IP layer. The TCP now breaks up the file into blocks of up to 1500 characters; these blocks are called **packets**. Each packet is then passed on to the IP layer, where it is prepared for transmission by adding header codes (explained above) that include the **destination address** (i.e. the client), the **source address** (i.e. the server) and the **time to live** (see page 99).

For the packet to travel from the server to the client, the digital signal must pass through several node points on the network. At each node point there is a memory store, where the packet is held for a time, and a circuit called a **router**, which examines the destination address of the packet. A router not only allows the packet of data to be transferred but also undertakes network traffic control. Routers continuously exchange information with each other about the most efficient route to take. If it is noticed that a broken link exists in the network then all routers will avoid using it. If packets arrive at a node point and fill up the memory faster than the router can empty it, then the excess packets are simply discarded. Discarded packets are eventually noticed at the end point by the TCP, which requests their retransmission.

Note that the pathway through the network for one packet from a file may not be the same as the pathway for another. Indeed, it is an interesting feature of the Internet that the order in which packets are sent may not be the same as the order in which they arrive. It is the TCP at the client that reassembles the packets into the original file. This is shown in *figure 11.6*.

Each packet of data has a time-to-live code number attached to the header. Each time the packet passes through a gateway, this number is reduced by one. If the packet has not reached its destination before this number is reduced to zero then it will be discarded. The code is necessary, because otherwise packets might loop around the nodes of a network forever.

Once these appropriately headed packets are ready for transmission, the server transmits one packet and waits for an acknowledgement from the client. When the acknowledgement arrives, the sender transmits two packets and waits for the client to respond with two acknowledgements. When these arrive, the sender transmits four packets and waits for four acknowledgements. Then the sender transmits eight packets and so on, continually increasing the number sent until the routers start to throw packets away. The TCP at the sender will notice the absence of acknowledgements and thus retransmit these packets until the entire file has been received.

Using the Internet via a phone line

Normally, a telephone call is a **connection-oriented** system, which effectively works in real time. That is to say, the two callers share the 'line' that connects them for as long as they wish to speak to each other.

The essential feature of the Internet, however, is that it is a **connectionless** system. That is to say, although the sender is transmitting information to the client they are not connected in real time. The information is broken up into packets and travels in bursts over different paths; transfers occur at different times, which are not controlled by either sender or client.

Access via a modem

For a home user to access the Internet through their telephone line, they must use a **modem**. A modem is a modulator and demodulator, which is required because the telephone line to the local exchange can only pass signals in the range 300 Hz to 3.4 kHz. The digital signals from the user's computer modulate an audio carrier in the modem by QAM (explained in chapter 4). The modem then passes the signal to the local exchange at a rate that depends on the quality of the wire-pair link. Some modems quote transfer rates of 56 k bit s^{-1} but, in practice, rates are often less than this. The audio signals that are returned to the user are demodulated by the modem and passed into the computer as a raw digital signal.

The signals from the modem allow the exchange to link the user to an **Internet service provider** (ISP), which is an organisation whose business is to allow users access to the Internet.

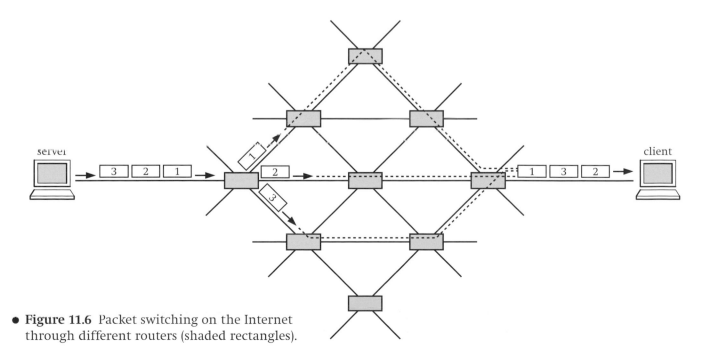

● **Figure 11.6** Packet switching on the Internet through different routers (shaded rectangles).

There are a large number of these businesses in the UK alone. A diagram of a home computer using the PTSN to connect to the Internet is shown in *figure 11.7*.

Using ordinary modems and telephone connections to access the Internet's huge store of graphics and other multimedia files can be frustratingly slow and it can sometimes take a long time to download the information required. If faster Internet access is required through the existing copper telephone cables then there are technologies that allow this.

Access via the ISDN system

The integrated services digital network (ISDN) is a technology that was developed in the 1980s but its use for Internet access has made it more popular. The telephone company will instal special digital switching equipment in the user's home and at their local exchange. Instead of a normal modem, the user will have a **terminal adapter**, which lets the user send and receive digital signals directly. There are several forms of ISDN access but the most common is known as **basic rate interface**. In this system, the user's telephone line is divided (by time-division multiplexing) into three channels. Two of these are $64\,\mathrm{kbit\,s^{-1}}$ **bearer channels** (B) and the other is a $16\,\mathrm{kbit\,s^{-1}}$ **data channel** (D). The D channel sends routing and control codes while the B channels communicate information. You can have a normal telephone conversation on one B channel while surfing the Internet on the other. It is also possible to combine the two B channels into a high-speed $128\,\mathrm{kbit\,s^{-1}}$ channel.

Access via the DSL system

Digital subscriber line (DSL) is a relatively new technology that allows the use of existing telephone lines to access the Internet at high bit rates. There are different forms of DSL available such as VDSL (very high speed DSL), which could allow data transfer rates as high as $55\,\mathrm{Mbit\,s^{-1}}$, although this system is very expensive and only likely to be installed by large organisations.

Because the DSL system uses existing copper telephone wires (in which the attenuation increases as the frequency increases), the user must be relatively close to the local exchange for the system to work. For example, at a rate of $8\,\mathrm{Mbit\,s^{-1}}$, the copper wires must be shorter than $3\,\mathrm{km}$. At a rate of $2\,\mathrm{Mbit\,s^{-1}}$, however, the copper wires can be up to $5\,\mathrm{km}$ in length.

An affordable system for normal home use is asymmetrical DSL (ADSL), where 'asymmetrical' refers to the fact that the rate at which data is received from the Internet is not the same as the rate at which data is transferred to it. ADSL requires a special electronic circuit in the user's home and a similar circuit at the other end of the line in the local exchange. The ADSL system divides the user's telephone line into three channels (by

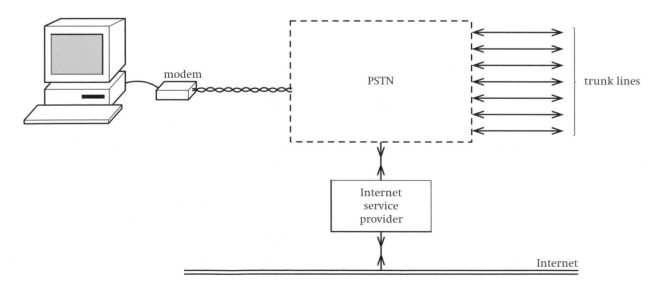

● **Figure 11.7** Accessing the Internet via a modem.

time-division multiplexing). One channel is used for normal telephone conversation, the second for sending data and the third for receiving data. Typically, data can be sent at a rate of $640\,\text{kbit s}^{-1}$ and received at a rate of $1.5\,\text{Mbit s}^{-1}$.

The World Wide Web

Until the appearance of the World Wide Web (WWW), the Internet was mainly used by people who had some computer expertise. File transfer protocol (FTP) was the standard method by which data could be stored on or removed from a server and if a document that had been transmitted had references to other documents then it was not straightforward to access them. In other words, FTP does not link separate documents together.

In 1992, Tim Berners-Lee, working at Europe's high-energy physics research centre in Switzerland, wrote the first **browser** program which used a protocol called **hypertext transfer protocol** (HTTP). This operates as follows:

When a client requests a Web server to send a document, the request is sent using HTTP (rather than FTP). The Web server finds the document in its memory and transmits it along with extra information. It is this extra information that distinguishes a Web server from an Internet server. The extra information transmitted is composed of two main parts:

- **control codes**, using **hypertext markup language** (HTML), by which the client computer screen can display the document, i.e. the layout, headings, bordering etc. Images can be transmitted as separate files and incorporated on the visible page by HTML code.
- **links** to other documents. These links are specific words or phrases in the text of the transmitted document that will allow related documents to be accessed.

When the mouse pointer of the client computer is moved over the document on the screen, the arrow changes to a hand with a pointing finger whenever it falls on any hypertext. If the user clicks on this link, the browser will automatically set up the link address and request the appropriate Web server to transmit the new document to the client. When this new document arrives, it is displayed on the screen.

A browser, therefore, is a program, stored in the client's computer, that is able to read hypertext.

While the Internet is the huge collection of computer networks and databases connected by backbone cable and optic fibre, the WWW is essentially a browsing and searching system. It allows users with virtually no expertise to access the information stored at certain sites on the Internet. These are sites that have been given web addresses and contain information deliberately put there by the people in charge of them. These sites can, in principle, be accessed without a knowledge of their address by using sophisticated computer programs called **search engines** (e.g. Yahoo, Lycos, Ask Jeeves). The search engines can be accessed through an Internet Service Provider.

The use of the Internet for multimedia

Originally, the Internet allowed the transfer of textual information only but it has now developed into a medium for the mass communication of images, sound clips, music, video and live radio and TV. This has become possible because of **file compression**. The importance of compressing information before transmission can be illustrated by the fact that a typical music CD would take more than a day to download through a modem that operated at a rate of $56\,\text{kbit s}^{-1}$.

SAQ 11.2

Calculate how long a modem operating at $56\,\text{kbit s}^{-1}$ would take to download all the bits stored on a normal CD containing one hour of stereo recorded music (stored as two 16-bit, left and right, samples taken 44 100 times per second).

Compression programs use algorithms, complex mathematical formulae, to shrink data files (i.e. to eliminate redundancies in any form of information so that an otherwise large file can be sent as a smaller number of bits). When the algorithm finds patterns in the data that repeat, then it replaces the pattern with a shorter, specific code. For example, a video image might contain a large section of blue sky, where the individual pixels will be the same colour over a large area. There is thus no need to transmit the same blue data over and over again for each pixel in the image.

Some examples of compression algorithms are:

- **MP3**

  This is a format that converts normal CD music into a compressed state while retaining high quality audio. A typical song occupies about 25 Mbits in MP3. After an MP3 file has been downloaded from the Internet, it can be played with a special piece of software called an MP3 player. Some Internet servers and software can **stream** the MP3 file, i.e. play it while it is being downloaded.

- **JPEG**

  Joint photographic experts group is a format that converts video images into a compressed state while retaining a high level of detail. With decompression software in the client computer, a decompression algorithm is run to reconstruct the original image. An entire Web page of text and graphics often corresponds to only 400 kbits or less.

- **GIF**

  Graphics interchange format is another commonly used system for compressing video images for transmission on the Internet. (Note that there are several other formats that have the same effect.)

- **MPEG**

  Motion picture experts group is a format that converts **moving** images into a state sufficiently compressed that, with the appropriate software, you can watch a video while it is being downloaded. This process is called **streaming video**.

How streaming audio works

When you use a Web browser to click on a sound clip on the Home page, the browser contacts the Web server, which returns a small text file containing the actual location on the Internet of the sound file you want to play, as well as instructions to activate your sound-player software. This player software contacts the audio server and communicates how fast the server can deliver the audio file (i.e. how fast your modem or line can swallow the compressed audio information). If you have a low-speed Internet connection then the sound quality will be poor. The server sends the audio in packets using the user datagram protocol (UDP) instead of the normal transmission control protocol (TCP). The important difference is that UDP does not keep re-sending packets if they are lost, as TCP does. (If TCP were used, your sound player could be constantly interrupted with late-arriving packets).

Telephone calls over the Internet

It is now possible to make a telephone call over the Internet. With a microphone and the appropriate hardware, your call will be digitised and compressed and broken up into packets for transmission using TCP/IP (i.e. both protocols). At the receiving computer, software decompresses the packets so that they can be played and heard. However, sometimes the packets will arrive out of order and thus appear to be missing. Under these circumstances, the software makes an estimate of the sound in the missing packet that has not yet arrived. (When the missing packet does arrive, the software discards it.)

SUMMARY

- A network is a set of links through which users communicate.

- The mesh network is the most versatile but also the most expensive.

- The Internet has evolved into a huge interconnection of computers. It works on the open systems interconnection (OSI) model.

- A protocol is a set of rules that govern some particular process.

- There are many protocols on the Internet.

- Data that is transferred over the Internet is arranged in packets.

- Each packet of data is preceded by header codes, containing the protocol in use.

- File transfer takes place through packet transfer and switching. Packets from the same file may not take the same route to the destination.

- Users access the Internet through an Internet service provider.

- DSL technology allows fast Internet access using existing telephone wires.

- The World Wide Web uses hypertext and browser programs, and hypertext transfer protocol (HTTP).

- The World Wide Web has enabled people without computer skills to have Internet access.

- The Internet is being increasingly used for multimedia purposes.

Questions

1 In a mesh network of four users, calculate the number of different routes through which a message can transferred from one user to another.

2 Explain what is meant by a protocol and why they are important to the Internet.

3 Explain the purpose of a router in file transfer and packet switching.

4 In what way is using the PSTN for a telephone call different from using the PSTN for Internet purposes?

5 Explain the difference between a document transfer by FTP and a document transfer by HTTP.

6 A security video camera has a picture composed of 90 lines and 120 pixels per line. Each pixel requires a five-bit code to store its brightness and colour. Calculate how many pictures per second can be communicated over the Internet if the user's modem can accept bits at a rate of $56 \, \text{kbit s}^{-1}$.

7 A user with ADSL Internet access receives bits at a rate of $1.5 \, \text{Mbit s}^{-1}$ through the copper wires from their local exchange. Calculate the maximum square wave frequency in the wires. Explain your working.

CHAPTER 12

The operational amplifier

By the end of this chapter you should be able to:

1 recall the characteristic properties of an ideal operational amplifier or *op-amp* in terms of *voltage gain*, *input resistance*, *output resistance* and *saturation levels*;

2 understand the behaviour of an op-amp in terms of producing an output voltage that depends on the difference between the two input voltages;

3 design circuits involving the use of an op-amp to provide a *switched response* to a gradual change in input voltage;

4 understand how the input voltage at which switching takes place may be changed;

5 understand the principles of *negative feedback* in an amplifier;

6 recall and explain the effect of negative feedback on the *gain* and on the *bandwidth* of an amplifier circuit;

7 recall the diagram for an *inverting amplifier* based on an op-amp;

8 understand that the inverting input of an inverting amplifier is known as a *virtual earth*;

9 use the virtual-earth approximation to derive an expression for the gain of an inverting amplifier with an ideal op-amp;

10 recall and use the expression for the voltage gain of an inverting amplifier;

11 design inverting amplifier circuits;

12 recall a simple input system for an optic fibre based on an amplifier using an op-amp and an LED;

13 recall a simple output system for an optic fibre based on an amplifier using an op-amp and a photodiode;

14 describe an experimental investigation of an optic-fibre system capable of communicating information, such as speech, over a short distance in a laboratory.

Introduction

The first integrated-circuit (IC) operational amplifier (**op-amp**) was designed by Bob Widlar and built by Fairchild Electronics in 1965. This device was a basic circuit unit from which analogue computers could be built. These programming devices were used in the 1960s and 1970s to solve mathematical equations by treating the variable under test as a voltage. The various terms in the equation became parts of an electronic circuit with each part mimicking a particular mathematical function. The op-amp is so called because it can be made to perform a number of mathematical operations, governed by the external circuitry chosen by the user.

Some of the operations that the op-amp can be made to perform are as follows:

■ comparison of two voltages;

- multiplication of a voltage by a constant;
- addition of two voltages;
- subtraction of two voltages;
- differentiation of a voltage with respect to time;
- integration of a voltage with respect to time.

Although analogue computers gradually lost their appeal (once digital computers became able to solve the same problem faster and with memory space) the versatile op-amp found a great many other uses in electronics.

The op-amp circuit symbol and a typical dual in line (DIL) package are shown in *figure 12.1*. The type shown is an 081, but it should be noted that there are hundreds of different types of op-amp being manufactured at the present time.

Of the eight pins on the IC, there are five with which most users are concerned. These are (*figure 12.2*):

pin 2, the inverting input – the voltage applied to it is called $V_{\text{inverting}}$;

pin 3, the non-inverting input – the voltage applied to it is called $V_{\text{non-inverting}}$;

pin 6, the output voltage V_{out};

pin 7, the positive supply line;

pin 4, the negative supply line.

Normally, op-amps are operated with a dual power supply and this requires three power lines, the positive supply line, the zero-volt line and the

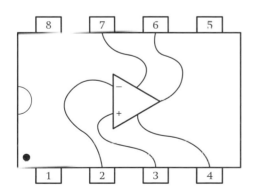

- **Figure 12.1** The dual in-line (DIL) package for an 081 op-amp.

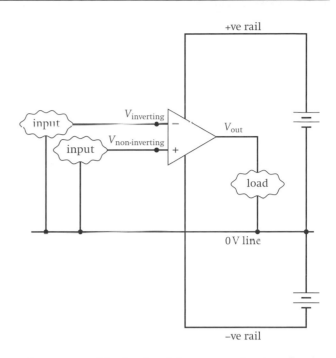

- **Figure 12.2** The basic wiring set up for an op-amp.

negative supply line (*figure 12.2*). The zero-volt (0 V) line is the reference against which all voltages are measured. Arranging the power supply in this way means that the output can drive a load positively or negatively. Thus, it could move the diaphragm of a loudspeaker both forwards and backwards, or it could make a small d.c. motor turn clockwise or anticlockwise.

Saturation of an op-amp

The op-amp is essentially a high-gain **differential amplifier**, i.e. the output voltage is the amplified difference between the two input voltages. The op-amp behaves according to the following formula:

$$V_{\text{out}} = A_0(V_{\text{non-inverting}} - V_{\text{inverting}})$$

where A_0 is a quantity known as the **open-loop gain**. For d.c. and low-frequency signals the open-loop gain is typically about 10^5.

To understand op-amp behaviour, we will calculate the output voltages of the three op-amps shown in *figure 12.3* overleaf, which are all being operated on ±15 V supplies.

a The inverting input is +2 V and the non-inverting input is +3 V. V_{out} is given by the operating equation:

$$V_{\text{out}} = 10^5 \times (3 - 2) = 100\,000 \text{ V}$$

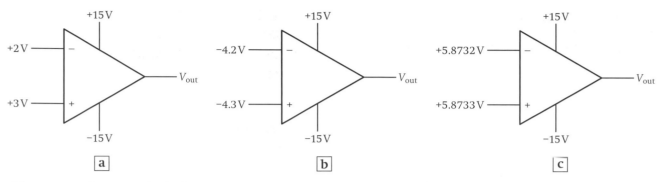

● **Figure 12.3** Op-amp calculations.

This voltage is enormously in excess of the positive supply line, so the output simply rises as high as it can go. This is **positive saturation**; V_{out} will be actually about +14 V on a +15 V supply.

b The inverting input is −4.2 V and the non-inverting input is −4.3 V. V_{out} is again given by the operating equation:

$$V_{out} = 10^5 \times [-4.3 - (-4.2)] = -10\,000 \text{ V}$$

This voltage is enormously below the negative supply line, so the output simply falls as low as it can. This is **negative saturation**; V_{out} will be about −14 V on a −15 V supply.

c The inverting input is +5.8732 V and the non-inverting input is +5.8733 V. V_{out} is given by the operating equation:

$$V_{out} = 10^5 \times (5.8733 - 5.8732) = +10 \text{ V}$$

Thus when an op-amp is **saturated**, the output voltage is as close to the voltage of one supply line as the internal circuitry will allow; the operating equation is no longer valid. When an op-amp output is not saturated, the reason can only be that the two inputs are nearly equal. This illustrates a fundamental rule for an op-amp.

> If the output is not saturated, then the two inputs must be virtually the same voltage.

Ideal and real op-amps

In designing operational amplifiers, engineers often produce an integrated circuit of about 20 or 30 transistors that has properties as closely matched as possible to those of an ideal differential amplifier. *Table 12.1* compares this ideal with those of typical real op-amps.

SAQ 12.1

An op-amp is powered by ± 15 V supplies. The non-inverting input voltage is −1.82 V and the inverting input is −1.79 V. What is the output voltage?

SAQ 12.2

An op-amp is powered by ± 15 V supplies. The non-inverting input voltage is +6.85 V and the output voltage is +5 V. Calculate the inverting input voltage, assuming that the open-loop gain is 10^5.

Property	Ideal op-amp	Real op-amp
input resistance	infinite, i.e. the two inputs drain no current from the circuit driving them	$10^6\,\Omega$ to $10^{12}\,\Omega$
output resistance	zero, i.e. the output can drive any load no matter how small its resistance	about $100\,\Omega$
voltage gain	infinite, and it will amplify any input frequency	10^5 to 10^6, depending on frequency
saturation level	the maximum and minimum voltages equal the supply line voltages	can only reach about 1 V less than the supply line voltages

● **Table 12.1** Comparing the properties of an ideal op-amp with those of a real op-amp.

Use as a comparator

The op-amp, when used in **open-loop mode**, i.e. without any feedback (see below), can be used as a **comparator**. This is a circuit that will **switch over** from one saturation level to the other when one of the input voltages changes with respect to the other. A simple example of this use of the op-amp is in a circuit that will operate a small lamp when it gets dark. This is shown in *figure 12.4*. The inverting and non-inverting inputs are derived from the two potential dividers, remembering that only very small currents flow to the inputs. The non-inverting input voltage depends on the light intensity reaching the light-dependent resistor (LDR). The inverting input is derived from two fixed resistors of 10 kΩ and 3.9 kΩ, so that this input is set at a fixed voltage of +2.5 V.

In daylight, the LDR's resistance may be only a few hundred ohms, so that the non-inverting input voltage is about 0.1 V. This causes the op-amp to be in negative saturation (i.e. output voltage ≈ −8 V). The diode will be reverse biased and so will prevent the small filament bulb from lighting up.

In darkness, the LDR's resistance may exceed 100 kΩ and this will cause the non-inverting input to rise beyond the fixed +2.5 V of the other input. Consequently, the output goes into positive saturation (i.e. output voltage ≈ +8 V) and the forward-biased diode allows the lamp to turn on fully.

Note that if the 10 kΩ resistor were replaced by a 10 kΩ variable resistor then the voltage, and thus the light intensity, at which switching takes place can be changed.

Use as an amplifier

In order to understand the use of the op-amp as an **amplifier**, it is important to remember that the open-loop gain A_o does not have the same value for all frequencies of input. Consider the circuit shown in *figure 12.5*, where the op-amp is being used in open-loop mode (with no feedback from the output to either input), to amplify the small a.c. signals from a signal generator. The input and output voltages can be displayed and measured on a dual-trace oscilloscope. (Note that normally the op-amp would not be used in this simple manner.)

To measure the **gain** of the amplifier at any input frequency, a sufficiently low input voltage must be applied, so that the output does not saturate (otherwise the calculation of gain would be invalid). The overall gain in this case would be just the open-loop gain A_o, calculated from the equation

$$A_o = \text{voltage gain} = \frac{\text{output voltage}}{\text{input voltage}}$$

The open-loop gain A_o is measured over a range of frequencies and then plotted on a logarithmic scale (to accommodate the large range of values of gain and frequency). The resulting graph, for an 081-type op-amp, is shown in *figure 12.6*. What is to be understood from this

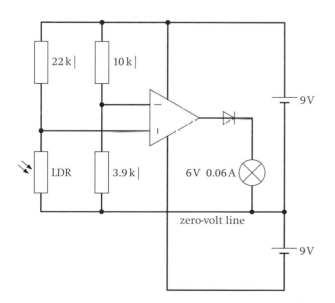

● **Figure 12.4** The op-amp as a comparator.

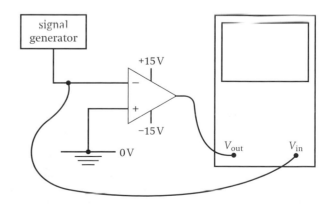

● **Figure 12.5** The op-amp used in open-loop mode.

plot – known as a characteristic – is that the op-amp can only be made to operate under, or inside, the graph and not outside it. For example, a user cannot build a circuit around this op-amp that will have a gain of 10^3 at a frequency of 10^5 Hz, because such an operating point occurs outside the characteristic. However, the user could build a circuit that will provide a gain of 10^3 at a frequency of 10^2Hz, because this operating point is inside the characteristic.

Note that the relatively cheap op-amps normally found in school laboratories provide very little gain at frequencies in the HF (i.e. MHz) range. It is possible to purchase high-speed op-amps that will operate in the VHF and UHF band but they are relatively expensive.

SAQ 12.3

With reference to the characteristic of *figure 12.6*, state whether it is possible to build an amplifier around an 081–type op-amp that will have a gain of 500 at a frequency of 200 kHz.

The effect of feedback on a general amplifier

In 1934, Harold Black devised the idea of adding **negative feedback** to an amplifier in order to improve the amplifier characteristics. To appreciate the effects, consider an amplifier as used in the two circuits of *figure 12.7*. In circuit *12.7a*, the amplifier is being used in the simple open-loop mode, so the voltage gain is A_o. In circuit *12.7b*, however, a fraction β of the output voltage is fed back to be added to the input voltage. In this case, the actual voltage gain of the amplifier is given by

$$A_o = \frac{\text{voltage produced at output}}{\text{voltage applied to input}} = \frac{V_{out}}{V_{in} + \beta V_{out}}$$

where in the second equation we incorporate the effect of feedback. Rearranging this equation produces

$$A_o(V_{in} + \beta V_{out}) = V_{out}$$
$$A_o V_{in} = (1 - \beta A_o)\, V_{out}$$

Thus the overall voltage gain G of the circuit is given by

$$G = \frac{V_{out}}{V_{in}} = \frac{A_o}{1 - \beta A_o}$$

If the fraction β is *positive* then the denominator in the above equation is less than 1 and the amplifier will have an enormous gain, so that it will be unstable and will saturate as fast as it can. Indeed, if $\beta A_o = 1$ then the amplifier can have an infinite gain and thus produce an output for virtually no input. Thus positive feedback

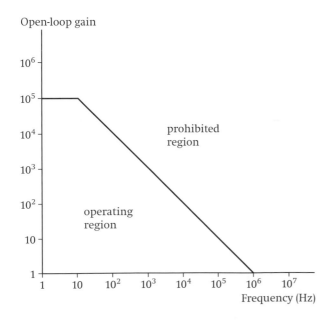

Open-loop gain

Figure 12.6 Open-loop frequency response of an op-amp.

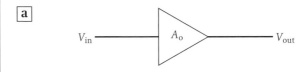

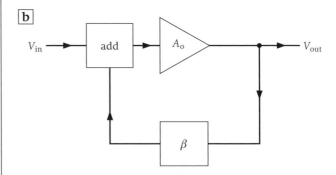

Figure 12.7 An amplifier **a** without, and **b** with feedback.

produces instability; this is the principle of oscillator circuits. The Schmitt trigger uses positive feedback to regenerate the signal at regular intervals in a long-distance cable.

If the fraction β is *negative*, then the denominator is greater than the numerator and the overall gain is less than the open-loop gain. If both the numerator and the denominator are divided by A_o then the overall gain becomes

$$G = \frac{1}{1/A_o - \beta}$$

If A_o is large then $1/A_o \sim 0$, and the overall gain depends *only* on the feedback fraction ($G = 1/\beta$) and not on the actual characteristic open-loop gain A_o of the amplifier. This is a major bonus for a circuit designer and is the principle reason that the open-loop gain of op-amps is so large (see below).

We should emphasise that the amplifier shown in *figure 12.7* is any general amplifier with a *single* input. One of the interesting features of an op-amp is that it is made with *two* inputs so that a designer can arrange positive or negative feedback with some ease. Any connection between the output and the non-inverting input will result in positive feedback and the amplifier will become unstable. Any connection between the output and the inverting input will result in negative feedback and this will produce accuracy and control. This is shown in the figure below.

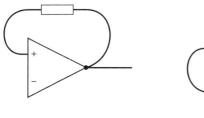
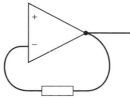

Positive feedback (instability)   Negative feedback (stability)

Negative feedback in op-amps

The essential principle of negative feedback is that the fraction of the output fed back to add to the input must be 180° out of phase with the input. In this way, the net input to the amplifier is reduced and so the overall output is reduced. There are two

basic circuits in which an op-amp is used as a voltage amplifier, and both of these circuits involve negative feedback. They are the **non-inverting amplifier** circuit and the **inverting amplifier** circuit, and both will be discussed below.

When an op-amp is used as a voltage amplifier, the input signal must never become large enough to cause the op-amp to saturate, otherwise **clipping distortion** is introduced and the formula for voltage gain is no longer valid. The combination of an unsaturated output and negative feedback causes the amplifier to work hard to keep the two inputs at virtually the same voltage.

The non-inverting amplifier

For a non-inverting amplifier, the inverting input is connected via a resistor R_f to the output terminal and via a resistor R_1 to the zero-volt line. This amplifier uses a potential divider to generate the feedback fraction β. The input voltage is applied to the non-inverting input and the feedback is applied via a resistor R_f to the inverting input (thus ensuring it is inverted, or 180° out of phase with the input signal). The circuit is shown in *figure 12.8*. Note that it is normal not to show the power lines.

Consider two methods of calculating the overall voltage gain for this amplifier, shown in *table 12.2*. *Figure 12.9* shows a sinusoidal input and the corresponding output for the amplifier of *figure 12.8*. The non-inverting nature of the amplifier is evident in the fact that the output voltage has the same phase as the input voltage (i.e. the output is not inverted). Note that the input resistance of

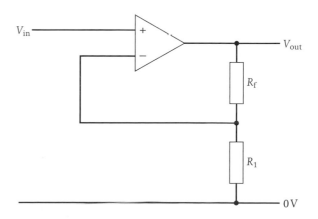

● **Figure 12.8** The non-inverting amplifier.

Gain from first principles	Gain from feedback fraction
The op-amp output must not saturate. Therefore we require $V_{in} = V_{non\text{-}inverting} = V_{inverting}$. Thus	The fraction of the output voltage fed back is β. Because the current in the feedback link is very small, the resistors form a potential divider, so
$$V_{in} = \frac{R_1}{R_1 + R_f} V_{out}$$	$$\beta = \frac{R_1}{R_1 + R_f}$$
and so $$\text{gain} = \frac{V_{out}}{V_{in}}$$ $$= \frac{R_1 + R_f}{R_1}$$ $$= 1 + \frac{R_f}{R_1}$$	Therefore $$\text{gain} = \frac{1}{\beta}$$ $$= \frac{R_1 + R_f}{R_1} = 1 + \frac{R_f}{R_1}$$

● **Table 12.2** The gain of a non-inverting amplifier.

this type of amplifier is very large, i.e. it draws very little current from the input source.

SAQ 12.4

Design a non-inverting amplifier with a voltage gain of 4.

The inverting amplifier

For an inverting amplifier, the non-inverting input is permanently wired to the zero-volt line. The

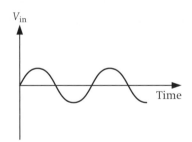

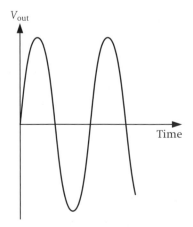

● **Figure 12.9** Input and output signals for a non-inverting amplifier.

input voltage is applied through a resistor R_1 to the inverting input and through a feedback resistor R_f to the output. The circuit is shown in *figure 12.10*.

The overall voltage gain of this amplifier may be calculated as follows. As for the non-inverting amplifier, the op-amp output must not saturate, therefore the two op-amp input voltages must be virtually the same. Thus

$$V_{inverting} \approx V_{non\text{-}inverting} = 0\,\text{V}$$

For this reason, the inverting input of this particular amplifier is often referred to as a **virtual earth** (earth potential is usually taken to be $0\,\text{V}$). In this **virtual-earth approximation**, when the inverting input can be taken as $0\,\text{V}$, to five significant figures, the input resistance of the amplifier is equal to the resistor R_1.

The current from the source of input voltage through the resistor R_1 must be equal to the current swallowed by the output voltage through

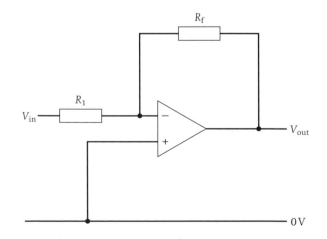

● **Figure 12.10** The inverting amplifier.

R_f, because the op-amp input itself drains virtually no current from the input source. Thus

input current = output current

and so

$$\frac{\text{p.d. across } R_1}{R_1} = \frac{\text{p.d. across } R_f}{R_f}$$

Therefore

$$\frac{V_{in} - 0}{R_1} = \frac{0 - V_{out}}{R_f}$$

Thus the voltage gain $= \dfrac{V_{out}}{V_{in}} = \dfrac{-R_f}{R_1}$

Figure 12.11 shows a sinusoidal input and the corresponding output for the amplifier of figure 12.10. The inverting nature of the amplifier is evident in the fact that the output voltage is 180° out of phase with the input voltage (i.e. the output is inverted).

SAQ 12.5

Design an inverting amplifier that has an input resistance of 68 kΩ and a voltage gain of –12.

Effect of gain on the amplifier bandwidth

It has already been noted, figure 12.6, that the open-loop gain A_o of a real op-amp is not constant with frequency and that the op-amp can only be operated in the region under this characteristic curve. The effects of this limitation on the design of amplifier gain and bandwidth are explained below. Although it is something of an approximation,

> ... the bandwidth of an amplifier may be taken to be the range of frequencies over which the maximum gain remains constant.

Suppose an inverting amplifier (figure 12.10 overleaf) is designed with a gain V_{out}/V_{in} equal to 10^3 (figure 12.12a). This can be achieved by making $R_f = 1\,M\Omega$ and $R_1 = 1\,k\Omega$. To plot the frequency response of this amplifier, a signal generator can be used as the input source and a dual-trace oscilloscope can be used to measure the input and output voltages. The voltage gain is calculated over a wide range of frequencies. The results are shown in figure 12.12. This amplifier will maintain a constant gain of 10^3 (its designed value) but only up to a frequency of 10^3 Hz, the point where the frequency response hits the open-loop characteristic of figure 12.6. The gain amplifier thus has a bandwidth of 10^3 Hz.

Now, suppose the inverting amplifier is redesigned with a gain of only 10 (figure 12.13a). This can be achieved by making $R_f = 10\,k\Omega$ and keeping $R_1 = 1\,k\Omega$. The frequency response may be measured as before and the results are shown in figure 12.13b. The redesigned amplifier will maintain a constant gain of 10 (its designed value) up to a greater frequency of 10^5 Hz, again the point where the frequency response hits the open-loop characteristic. The amplifier thus has a bandwidth of 10^5 Hz.

Thus, as the gain is reduced the bandwidth is increased and, for op-amps of the 081 type, the product of designed gain and resulting bandwidth is a constant known as the **gain–bandwidth product** (it has a value of about 10^6):

designed gain × resulting bandwidth ≈ 10^6 Hz

Summary of effects of negative feedback
- The designed amplifier gain is less than the open-loop gain, and is otherwise independent of the open-loop gain.

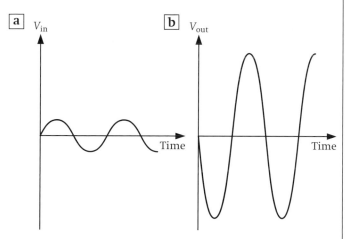

• **Figure 12.11 a** Input and **b** output signals for an inverting amplifier.

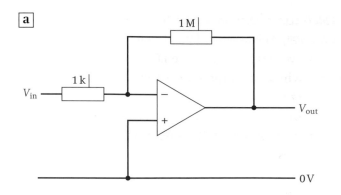

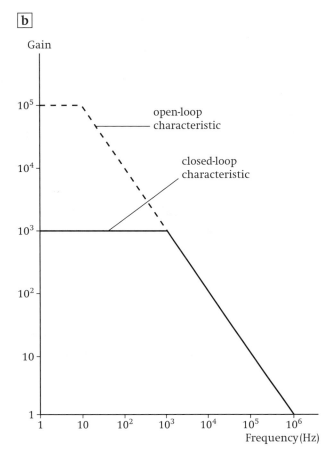

● **Figure 12.12 a** An inverting amplifier with a closed-loop gain of 10^3; **b** its frequency response.

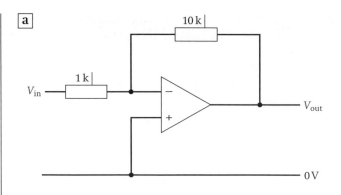

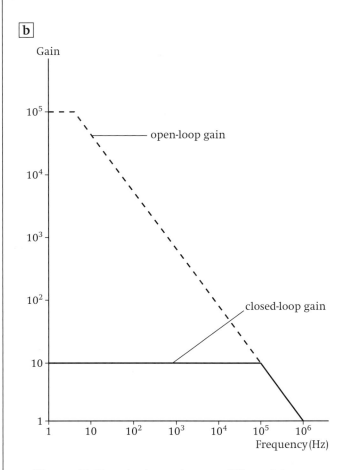

● **Figure 12.13 a** An inverting amplifier with a closed-loop gain of 10; **b** its frequency response.

■ The lower the designed gain, the greater is the corresponding bandwidth.
■ The amplifier is more stable (i.e. less likely to go into oscillation).
■ There is less distortion (i.e. the output is a better copy of the input).
Note that if it is required to build an amplifier with an overall gain of 10^3 with a bandwidth of

10^5 Hz, then *three* op-amps, each with a gain of 10 (and a bandwidth of 10^5 Hz) can be cascaded.

SAQ 12.6

Calculate the bandwidth of an inverting amplifier, built around an 081–type op–amp, which has a 1.5 kΩ input resistor and a 390 kΩ feedback resistor.

Op-amps and optic-fibre audio communication

It is possible to communicate speech or music in the laboratory as an analogue signal in an optic fibre. Relatively cheap and large-diameter plastic fibres and couplings can be purchased from several electronic suppliers, together with the other components described in the circuit below.

The transmitter

An audio frequency signal from a cheap crystal microphone is applied to the input of the non-inverting amplifier shown in *figure 12.14*. Suppose the microphone output is of the order of ± 20 mV and suppose it is desired that the output voltage should wobble by about ± 2 V. This means that the amplifier must be designed to have a voltage gain of about 2/0.02 = 100. In fact, the non-inverting amplifier in the transmitting circuit has a gain of 1 + 100/1 = 101.

The transmitter amplifier drives an LED, and it should be noted that the cathode of this device is connected to the negative rail and not the 0 V line. The reason is that a connection to the 0 V line would only allow the diode to turn on when the output voltage was greater than about + 1.7 V (i.e. for most of the time the diode would be off, and the light would be emitted in brief bursts when the output happened to rise above the 1.7 V turn-on level). With the cathode connected to the negative rail, however, the LED is on all the time, even when no sound enters the microphone. During silence, the amplifier output is 0 V and the current in the LED (known as the quiescent current) is given by the ratio of the p.d. across the series resistor to its resistance:

$$\text{quiescent LED current} = \frac{6 - 1.7}{470} \approx 9 \text{ mA}$$

When the sound reaches a suitable level, the microphone generates a signal of about ±20 mV and, consequently, the amplifier output changes by about ±2 V. This 2 V wobble causes the current in the LED to fluctuate by about ±4 mA (i.e. between 13 mA and 5 mA) and this in turn causes the light intensity output from the LED to vary in sympathy with the sound input.

The fact that the LED is on all the time means that the variation in light intensity is analogous to the original audio signal. The light signal has thus become an amplitude-modulated carrier.

The receiver

The non-inverting receiver amplifier is shown on the right in *figure 12.14*. The light intensity from the fibre is made to fall on a photodiode in reverse bias. The photodiode is part of a potential divider

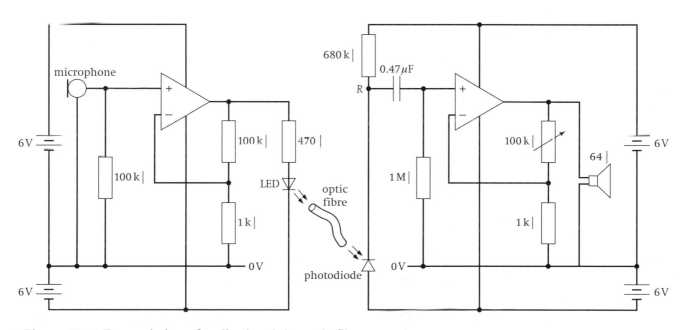

● **Figure 12.14** Transmission of audio signals by optic fibre.

made up with a fixed resistor of several hundred kΩ. As mentioned earlier, in the dark the photo-diode passes no current, but once the fluctuating light falls on it, a fluctuating d.c. current flows. This fluctuating current causes a fluctuating voltage across the 680 kΩ resistor (experimentation might be required with the value of this resistor for some diodes).

The actual d.c. voltage at point R is not important since only the wobbles in voltage carry the audio information. Consequently, a capacitor is used to block the d.c. and let through the a.c. wobble to the receiver amplifier.

By varying the wiper position on the 100 kΩ variable resistor, the receiving op-amp can have a maximum voltage gain of $(1\,k\Omega + 100\,k\Omega)/1k\Omega = 101$

and a minimum voltage gain of 1. This should allow enough control for an acceptable sound level from the small 64 Ω loudspeaker.

Note that if a photodiode is not available then a light-dependent resistor (LDR), suitably shielded from the normal light in the laboratory, will do, but then the 680 kΩ resistor in the potential divider should be replaced with a 10 kΩ resistor. Note also that the effective frequency response of an LDR is limited to just a few kHz, because it is very slow to respond to fast-changing light signals.

Even if an optic fibre is not available, the circuit will still transmit and receive through a vacuum or air (provided the transmitter and receiver are not too far apart).

SUMMARY

◆ The op-amp is a high open-loop-gain differential amplifier: it amplifies the difference in voltage between its two inputs.

◆ Saturation occurs when an op-amp output is as positive or as negative as it can get.

◆ If the output is not saturated, then the two inputs must be virtually equal.

◆ Real op-amps have characteristics similar to ideal op-amps.

◆ The op-amp may be used as a comparator or switch-over system to compare two voltages.

◆ The open-loop gain of a real op-amp falls as the frequency increases.

◆ Positive feedback produces instability.

◆ Negative feedback produces stability.

◆ Both inverting and non-inverting amplifiers involve negative feedback.

◆ Negative feedback reduces the gain but increases the bandwidth.

◆ Op-amps can be used with optic fibres to communicate audio signals.

Questions

1 Design a simple comparator circuit (*figure 12.4*) that will switch on a red LED when the temperature is above a certain value and switch on a green LED when the temperature is below it. You should use a potential divider with a negative temperature coefficient (n.t.c.) thermistor, which has a resistance that decreases when the temperature rises.

2 Design a non-inverting amplifier with a gain of 40. Calculate the bandwidth of this amplifier.

3 Design an inverting amplifier that has an input resistance of 20 kΩ and a gain of −34. Calculate the bandwidth of this amplifier.

4 An inverting amplifier has an input resistor of 10 kΩ and a feedback resistor of 220 kΩ. It is run on power supply lines of ±15 V. Calculate the maximum voltage that should be applied to this amplifier if it is not to saturate.

5. A non-inverting amplifier is made from two resistors, 153 kΩ and 75 kΩ, with the larger resistor as the feedback resistor. The power lines are ±15 V. Calculate the voltage gain, the bandwidth and the maximum input signal if saturation is to be avoided.

Answers to questions

Chapter 1

Self-assessment questions

1.1   In Braille, flat paper is modulated by raised dots. Each letter has a unique code of dots.

1.2   The most commonly occurring letters are given the shortest codes. This minimises the number of dots and dashes per message and thus minimises the transmission time.

1.3   At that time there was no communication system over water other than by ship. This could take several days. An electrically operated cable could reduce the communication time to an instant.

1.4   In a string telephone, the voice is transmitted as modulated longitudinal waves along the taut string. In an electrical telephone, the voice is transmitted as a modulated d.c. current in a pair of wires.

End-of-chapter questions

1   The a.c. mains normally has a constant frequency and a constant amplitude and this constancy means there is no information present (although there have been attempts to pass telephone signals via the mains grid).

2   Suppose the Guide can change her hand positions once per second. Suppose also that there are on average five letters per word. The transmission time would then be 1200 × 1000 × 5 × 1 seconds ≈ 70 days.

3   Copper cable was expensive and using the Earth as a return saved the cost of a return cable.

4   The original telephone required direct wiring between users (no exchange); laying a long-distance cable for only two users would have been too expensive (no multiplexing); the high cost meant only a limited number of customers.

5   Point-to-point communication refers to a transmission channel with a single user at either end. Broadcasting refers to information transfer from one source to an unknown number of users.

Chapter 2

Self-assessment questions

2.1

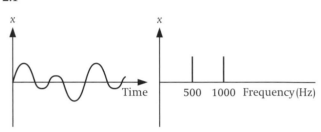

2.2   The security video bandwidth = (400/2) × 300 × 2 = 120 kHz.

2.3   It will be an analogue signal. The output p.d. will vary continuously as the temperature changes.

2.4   **a** Decimal 49 = 110001 in binary.
b Binary 100110 = decimal 38.

End-of-chapter questions

1   Wavelength = 330 / 440 = 0.75 m.

2   Frequency = $3 \times 10^8 / 0.06$ = 5 GHz.

3   Bandwidth = 8.0 kHz.

4   Number of output states = 2^8 = 256.

5   Quantisation error
$$= \frac{\text{voltage range}}{\text{number of outputs}} = 9 / 2^{16} = 0.14 \text{ mV}.$$

Chapter 3

Self-assessment questions

3.1

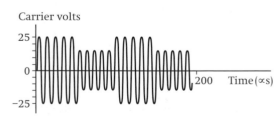

3.2   Bandwidth of FM waveform = 2 × (32 + 8) = 80 kHz.

Questions

1 AM carrier frequency = $1 / 10\,\mu s$ = 100 kHz.
Pure tone frequency = $1 / 100\,\mu s$ = 10 kHz.

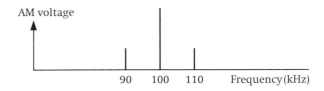

2

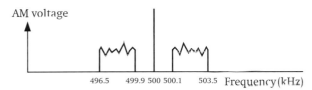

Bandwidth of AM station = 2×3.5 = 7 kHz.

3 FM radio requires a bandwidth of 180 kHz.
Therefore only one FM station could operate in
the LW waveband.

4 FM carrier frequency = $1 / 1\,\mu s$ = 1 MHz
Pure tone frequency = $1 / 10\,\mu s$ = 100 kHz.

5 Frequency deviation of FM carrier,
$\Delta f_c = 3 \times 10$ = 30 kHz.
Bandwidth of FM signal = $2 \times (30 + 4)$ = 68 kHz.

Chapter 4

Self-assessment questions

4.1 The sampling frequency could be 9.8 kHz or
18 kHz, according to the Nyquist criterion.

4.2 Data-logger bit rate = 200×12 = 2400 bit s⁻¹.
Total number of bits stored = $30 \times 200 \times 12$
= 72 000.

End-of-chapter questions

1 The lowest possible sampling frequency is 11 MHz.

2 Total number of bits = $15 \times 60 \times 8000 \times 8$
= 5.76×10^{7}.

3 Bit rate = 2000×4 = 8000 bit s⁻¹.
The maximum bit duration = $1 / 8000$ = 0.125 ms.

4 If the bit order is 101010101010 etc., then
10 kbit s⁻¹ produce a (rounded off) frequency of
5 kHz.

5 Bit rate = $1 /$ bit duration = $1 /$ time for four cycles
of 4.8 kHz or $1 /$ time for two cycles of 2.4 kHz
= 1200 Hz.

6 Baud rate = $1 / 20\,\mu s$ = 50 000 symbols s⁻¹.

Bit rate = $4 \times 50\,000$ = 200 000 bit s⁻¹.

Chapter 5

Self-assessment questions

5.1 $P = 42 \times 10^{1.6}$ = 1672.

5.2 Number of decibels = $10\,\lg (5 \times 10^{-7} / 1.0 \times 10^{-12})$
= 57 dB.

5.3 **a** Total power loss in cable = 100×8 = 800 dB.

b Total gain in amplifiers = 20×41 = 820 dB.

c Overall signal gain = $820 - 800$ = 20 dB.

Thus $10\,\lg (P_{out} / P_{in})$ = 20, so $\lg (P_{out} / P_{in})$ = 2, P_{out}
= $P_{in} \times 10^{2}$ and so output signal = $200\,mW \times 10^{2}$
= 20 W.

End-of-chapter questions

1 Output power of amplifier = $25 \times 10^{-6} \times 10^{3.6}$
= 0.1 W.

2 60 dB is equivalent to 10^{6} times greater.

3 35 dB = $10\,\lg (P_{signal} / P_{noise})$ so $P_{signal} / P_{noise} = 10^{3.5}$.
Therefore $P_{signal} = 8 \times 10^{-6} \times 10^{3.5}$ = 0.0253 W.
Maximum allowable attenuation of cable
= $10\,\lg (0.0253 / 2.8)$ = −20.4 dB.
Therefore maximum uninterrupted length
= $-20.4 / 6.8$ = 3.0 km.

4 Total attenuation of cable = 4.2×15 = 63 dB.
Total change in signal = $60 - 63$ = −3 dB.
Emerging signal power = $64 \times 10^{-0.3}$ = 32 mW.

Chapter 6

Self-assessment questions

6.1 Maximum number of TV stations = $(480 - 360) / 8$
= 15.

6.2 Wavelength of transmission = $3 \times 10^{8} / 150 \times 10^{6}$
= 2 m.

The dipole must be composed of two rods each
0.5 m in length.

End-of-chapter questions

1 Without multiplexing, each long-distance (trunk)
line would be tied up with only one call at a
time; laying many parallel long-distance lines to
accommodate many users would be prohibitively
expensive. The telephone system would therefore
be greatly restricted because of cost.

2 FM generates a wider bandwidth than AM, and at lower frequencies there is very limited bandwidth available; FM transmissions on these frequencies would severely limit the number of potential users.

3 The width of the HF band is from 3 MHz to 30 MHz. Thus the maximum number of radio amateurs = $27 \times 10^6 / 4 \times 10^3 = 6750$ (allowing no frequency space between transmissions and ignoring the use of the waveband for other purposes).

4 Wavelength = $3 \times 10^8 / 375 \times 10^6 = 0.8$ m. The dipole should be of total length 0.4 m.

5 A typical MF waveband frequency is about 2 MHz. The wavelength of transmission = $3 \times 10^8 / 2 \times 10^6$ = 150 m. A half-wave dipole would therefore be 75 m long, which is not portable.

6 A mobile-phone network operates on UHF and SHF wavebands, with wavelengths of the order of centimetres. The aerial size is thus also of the order of centimetres.

7 Parabolic dish aerials cannot be made omnidirectional; they can only transmit to and receive from a limited direction. Furthermore, they would be too large to be practical in the lower-frequency wavebands.

Chapter 7

Self-assessment questions

7.1 **a** Skip distance = $2 \times 200 \div \tan 30 \approx 700$ km.

7.2 **b** The angle subtended (from the centre of the Earth) between A and B is θ, where $\cos \theta = 6\,400\,000 / 6\,400\,100$; thus $\theta = 0.3203°$ = 5.59×10^{-3} radians.

Range = length of arc subtended = $R \times \theta = 35.8$ km.

(You could use Pythagoras and calculate $\sqrt{(6\,400\,100^2 - 6\,400\,000^2)} = 35.8$ km.)

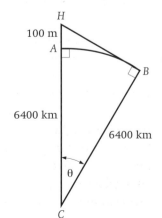

End-of-chapter questions

1 The AM transmitter uses $\lambda = 3000$ m, so waves will easily diffract around the base of the hill. The FM transmitter uses $\lambda = 3$ m, so limited-diffraction, or line-of-sight, transmission results and the hill will create a shadow.

2 The transatlantic carrier waves could have been supplied by a powerful transmitter in the LF waveband, so that the waves would bend around the ocean (surface waves).

Alternatively, the carrier frequency could have been in the HF waveband, so that sky waves would make multiple reflections between the ionosphere and the sea.

3 French TV uses carriers in the UHF and SHF wavebands, with a line-of-sight range of order 40 km. French radio, on the LF, MF and HF wavebands, propagates for hundreds of kilometres so is easily picked up in London.

4 Approximate area of USA = 3000×2000
= 6×10^6 km^2.
Assume area covered by each transmitter is a 25 km radius circle, area ≈ 2000 km^2.
Thus number of transmitters required
≈ $6 \times 10^6 / 2000 \approx 3000$.

5 The detector is also known as a demodulator: its function is to remove the carrier wave, thus yielding the information audio signal. It is usually a solid-state diode, which only conducts on one half-cycle of the signal. After passing through the diode, the average received signal is no longer zero, so the carrier can be filtered out by a smoothing circuit.

Chapter 8

Self-assessment questions

8.1 Area of solar cells = $(100/1500) \times 5\% = 1.67$ m^2

8.2 Satellite speed = $\sqrt{GM/r}$
= $\sqrt{6.7 \times 10^{-11} \times 6.0 \times 10^{24} / 7600 \times 10^3}$
= $\sqrt{\dfrac{6.7 \times 6.0 \times 10^7}{7.6}}$ = 7.27×10^3 m s^{-1}
= 7.27 km s^{-1} = 2.62×10^4 km h^{-1}
= 1.63×10^4 mph

Satellite period = $\dfrac{2\pi r}{v} = \dfrac{2\pi \times 7600 \text{ km}}{7.25 \text{ km s}^{-1}}$
= 6600 s
= 110 minutes

8.3 To find the angular limit in latitude, α, use the triangle CSA: $\cos \alpha = r/R$, so $\alpha = \cos^{-1}(6400/42000)$ = 81°.

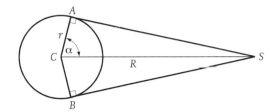

End-of-chapter questions

1 The satellite does not require a large array of solar cells because it only transmits for a few minutes per day. The transmission distance from a low Earth orbit is only a few hundred kilometres, so a powerful transmitter is not required. The wavelength of 150 MHz is 2 m, so a parabolic dish would have to be large and, as the satellite is moving, the dish would have to move to track it. A relatively fast and steerable dish of about 20 m in diameter would be prohibitively expensive, but a Yagi array is suitable.

2 Maximum power received
$$= \frac{\text{area of dish}}{\text{area of footprint}} \times 250\,\text{W}$$
$$= \frac{\pi \times (0.75)^2}{\pi \times (350\,000)^2} \times 250 = 1.15\,\text{nW}$$

3 Signal power received $= 1800 \times 10^{-18}$
$$= 1.8 \times 10^{-15}\,\text{W}$$

4 Transit time for signal $= \dfrac{\text{distance travelled}}{\text{speed of light}}$
$$= \frac{2 \times 36\,000 \times 10^3}{3 \times 10^8}$$
$$= 0.24\ \text{second}$$

5 If more than one satellite link were involved in a long-distance telephone call then there would be a time delay of the order of 0.5 second or more. Conversation under such circumstances could be frustrating.

Chapter 9

Self-assessment questions

9.1 Key 3 generates 687 Hz and 1477 Hz.

9.2 As soon as the handset is picked up there is a d.c. connection to the exchange. Thus as soon as the exchange notices the flow of d.c. current, it stops sending 50 V pulses.

9.3 Time between samples

= 1/sampling frequency = 1/8000 Hz
= 0.000125 s = 125 μs

9.4 Maximum number of downlink carrier frequencies available to the system
$$= \frac{\frac{1}{2}(1.99 - 1.85)\,\text{GHz}}{200\,\text{kHz}} = 350$$

End-of-chapter questions

1 Two people can be chosen from 10 in 10 × 9/2 ways. Thus the 10 independent users need 45 lines.

2 The user's line *to* the local exchange is reserved for the exclusive use of that user. The trunk line *from* the exchange has to be shared by many users.

3 Coaxial cable can be buried underground (this was not practical with open wires, which had to be kept separate). It greatly reduces crosstalk, so that there is less interference from other cables. It has a smaller attenuation, so high-frequency signals can be sent further before amplification is necessary. It has a greater bandwidth, so many more calls can be multiplexed together.

4 Number of bits produced by call
$= 25 \times 60 \times 8000 \times 8 = 9.6 \times 10^7$
Time of use of line
$= 9.6 \times 10^7 \times 0.02 \times 10^{-6} = 1.92$ seconds

5 If the mobile-phone cell radius were 50 km, the handset transmitter would have to be significantly more powerful. A more powerful microwave transmitter repeatedly held at the head might produce biological damage.

Chapter 10

Self-assessment questions

10.1 $1.500 \sin i_c = 1.485 \sin 90°$, so $\sin i_c = 1.485/1.500 = 0.99$. Thus $i_c = 82°$.

10.2 **a** Speed of light in fibre $= 3 \times 10^8/1.5$
$= 2 \times 10^8\,\text{m s}^{-1}$.
Time down central axis $= 6000/(2 \times 10^8) = 30\,\mu\text{s}$.
b Ray reflecting at critical angle travels a distance of $6000/\sin 82° = 6060\,\text{m}$.
Travel time for reflecting ray $= 6060/(2 \times 10^8)$
$= 30.3\,\mu\text{s}$.

10.3 The LED is not used as a light source in monomode fibres for two reasons: it cannot inject enough light power into the tiny 9 μm diameter core; LED light, which comprises a range of wavelengths, will suffer material dispersion.

End-of-chapter questions

1 Speed of light in fibre = $3 \times 10^8 / 1.5 = 2 \times 10^8 \, \text{m s}^{-1}$.
Time delay = $6000 \times 10^3 / 2 \times 10^8 = 0.03$ second.

2 Total attenuation = $15 \times 0.3 = 4.5 \, \text{dB}$. So $4.5 = 10 \lg (P_L / P_R)$, and if $P_L = 2 \, \text{mW}$ then the received light power $P_R = 2 \times 10^{-0.45} = 0.71 \, \text{mW}$.

3 Total attenuation = $35 \times 0.2 = 7.0 \, \text{dB}$. So $7.0 = 10 \lg (P_L / P_R)$, and if $P_L = 30 \, \text{mW}$ then the emerging light power $P_R = 30 \times 10^{-0.7} = 6 \, \text{mW}$. If the signal-to-noise ratio is $28 \, \text{dB}$ then the noise power P_N is given by $28 = 10 \lg (P_R / P_N)$.
Thus $P_N = 6 \times 10^{-2.8} = 9.5 \, \mu\text{W}$

4 Electric motors generally radiate a significant amount of electromagnetic power. Normal copper conductors would pick this up as noise due to interference. Optic fibres are immune to such interference.

Chapter 11

Self-assessment questions

11.1 a Total length of cable for mesh network
= $4 \times 100 + 2 \times 141 = 683 \, \text{m}$

b Total length of cable for star network
= $2 \times 141 = 283 \, \text{m}$

c Total length of cable for ring network
= $4 \times 100 = 400 \, \text{m}$

11.2 Download time
= $(60 \times 60 \times 44100 \times 2 \times 16) \div (56 \times 1000)$ seconds
= 25.2 hours

End-of-chapter questions

1 For a mesh network of four users there are five different possible routes from any one user to any other.

2 A protocol is set of rules governing a communication process: each different process operates according to a particular protocol. As the Internet allows the communication of information in many forms through many network nodes then protocols are essential to make the system work.

3 A router is an electronic circuit controlling the transfer of packets of information through the nodes of a network. Routers examine addresses and decide the most efficient route through which to transfer the packet.

4 A telephone call uses a connection-oriented system where the line between one telephone and another is shared for the entire duration of the call. The Internet is a connectionless system with no fixed line linking the server and client.

5 Document transfer by FTP does not provide links to other documents whereas HTTP does.

6 The bit rate required for each frame
= $90 \times 120 \times 5 = 54\,000 \, \text{bit s}^{-1}$.

Thus number of frames per second
= $56\,000 \div 54\,000 \approx 1$.

7 If the arrangement of bits is 1010101010 etc. then the maximum frequency of the corresponding square wave is $1.5 \times 10^6 \div 2 = 750\,000 \, \text{Hz}$.

Chapter 12

Self-assessment questions

12.1 Output voltage $\approx -14 \, \text{V}$.

12.2 Inverting input voltage = $6.85 - 5/10^5 = 6.849\,95 \, \text{V}$.

12.3 No. The operating point would lie outside the characteristic.

12.4 *Figure 12.8* with $R_f = 30 \, \text{k}\Omega$ and $R_1 = 10 \, \text{k}\Omega$.

12.5 *Figure 12.10* with $R_1 = 68 \, \text{k}\Omega$ and $R_f = 820 \, \text{k}\Omega$.

12.6 Gain of inverting amplifier = $-390 / 1.5 = -260$.
Bandwidth of amplifier = $10^6 \, \text{Hz} / 260 = 3850 \, \text{Hz}$.

End-of-chapter questions

1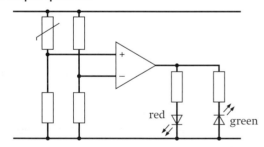

2 *Figure 12.8* with $R_f = 390 \, \text{k}\Omega$ and $R_1 = 10 \, \text{k}\Omega$.
Bandwidth = $10^6 \, \text{Hz} / 40 = 25 \, \text{kHz}$.

3 *Figure 12.10* with $R_1 = 20 \, \text{k}\Omega$ and $R_f = 680 \, \text{k}\Omega$.
Bandwidth = $10^6 \, \text{Hz} / 34 = 29.4 \, \text{kHz}$.

4 The maximum output voltage must be $14 \, \text{V}$. Since the gain is -22, the maximum input voltage
= maximum output voltage/gain = $14 / 22 = 0.64 \, \text{V}$.

5 Voltage gain = $1 + 75 / 15 = 6$.
Bandwidth = $10^6 / 6 \, \text{Hz} = 167 \, \text{kHz}$.
Maximum input voltage
= maximum output voltage/gain = $\pm 14 / 6 = 2.33 \, \text{V}$.

Glossary

alias a false signal generated as a result of sampling at too low a frequency

amplitude modulation the process by which the amplitude of a high-frequency carrier wave is controlled by the instantaneous value of a lower frequency information signal

analogue signal a voltage which varies in time in an analogous manner to the physical property which generated it; can have any value between two limits

analogue-to-digital electronic process which converts voltage samples into binary numbers or codes

attenuation the gradual loss in energy or power of a signal as it passes through a transmission medium

bandwidth the range of frequencies present in a signal or the range of frequencies a transmission medium will pass

baseband the range of frequencies in the information signal

channel the information pathway within a transmission medium; by means of multiplexing, many channels can be accommodated within one single medium (wire pair, coaxial cable, optic fibre or atmosphere)

critical angle the minimum angle of incidence required to cause total internal reflection

cross-talk (cross-linking) radiation picked up from adjacent signals

decibel a unit for comparing two powers (number of dB = $10 \lg P_1/P_2$)

demodulation the process of removing the carrier and extracting the information

digital signal a coded representation of a piece of information; voltage can only have one of two values

digital-to-analogue the electronic process which converts binary codes into an equivalent analogue voltage

dipole a basic aerial composed of two rods or tubes each of quarter wavelength

dispersion the process by which different rays from the same light pulse take different times to travel down an optic fibre; depends on both wavelength and pathlength

e-mail a half-duplex message service between two computers

fading a decrease in signal strength at a receiver when waves arrive by two or more different paths

frequency-division multiplexing the process of allocating to a number of users different carrier frequencies within the bandwidth of a transmission medium

frequency modulation the process by which the frequency of a high frequency carrier wave is controlled by the instantaneous value of a lower frequency information signal

gain a measure of the output power from an amplifier compared to the input power

geostationary satellite a satellite which appears not to move relative to an observer on Earth; used for weather monitoring, microwave links and TV broadcasting

graded-index fibre a type of optic fibre where the core is made with a refractive index which gradually increases towards the centre

ground wave a combination of the surface wave and the space wave in the LF and MF wavebands

ionosphere a region of low density ionised gases in the upper atmosphere of Earth

Internet an interconnection of packet networks operated by various industries, universities and governments around the world

keying the process of modulating a continuous wave carrier with digital data

mobile phone a system where part of the path between handset and exchange is completed by radio waves

modulation the process of varying some property of a carrier wave to allow it to carry information

monomode fibre a type of optic fibre where the diameter of the core is extremely narrow so that only one light path (or mode) can be followed; eliminates multipath dispersion

multimode fibre a type of optic fibre where the diameter of the core is relatively large allowing many different light paths (or modes); causes serious multipath dispersion

multiplexing the process of allowing several users to share the same transmission medium

negative feedback a fraction of the output voltage of an amplifier which is 180° out of phase with the input voltage is added to the input voltage; results in decreased gain, increased bandwidth and greater stability

noise the sum of all the unwanted energy which is added to the information signal

Nyquist's theorem the sampling frequency in a PCM system must be at least twice the highest frequency in the information signal

op-amp a small integrated circuit package which can be made to perform various mathematical operations on input voltages

parabolic dish aerial a dish shaped according to $y \propto x^2$ where parallel waves are made to reflect to a focus on a small aerial; used to increase signal-to-noise ratio

polar orbiting satellite a satellite in low Earth orbit over North and South Poles; used for monitoring the planet for geology, meteorology and military purposes

protocols a set of rules governing the way telecommunication links are set up and data is transferred

pulse code modulation the process of sampling an information signal and converting each sample into a n-bit binary word; the n bits are then transmitted in series, sample after sample, as a digital signal by keying some carrier

sidebands the frequencies generated on either side of a continuous wave carrier when it is modulated (either by AM or FM) by an information signal

signal-to-noise ratio the ratio (expressed in dB) of the signal power to noise power

sky wave any wave in the HF band which propagates by repeated reflections between the ionosphere and the surface of the Earth

space wave any wave in the HF, VHF, UHF, SHF, or EHF wavebands which propagates by line of sight

surface wave any wave in the LF and MF waveband which propagates by curving around the Earth's surface

time-division multiplexing the process by which a number of users are allocated the entire bandwidth of a transmission medium but at different periods of time

time-slot switching the process by which modern telephone exchanges operate

Index